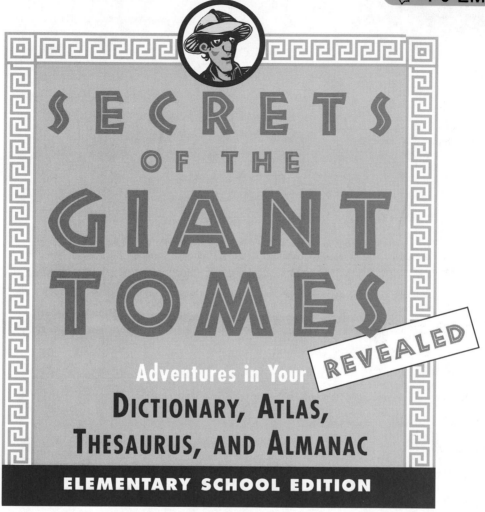

SECRETS OF THE GIANT TOMES REVEALED

Adventures in Your DICTIONARY, ATLAS, THESAURUS, AND ALMANAC

ELEMENTARY SCHOOL EDITION

BY CHRIS KENSLER

A Paper Airplane Project

Simon & Schuster

New York • London • Sydney • Singapore • Toronto

Kaplan Publishing
Published by Simon & Schuster, Inc.
1230 Avenue of the Americas
New York, NY 10020

For bulk sales to schools, colleges, and universities, please contact: Order Department, Simon & Schuster, 100 Front Street, Riverside, NJ 08075. Phone: 1-800-223-2336. Fax: 1-800-943-9831.

Kaplan® is a registered trademark of Kaplan, Inc.

Cover Design: Cheung Tai
Cover Illustration: Jeff Foster
Interior Page Design and Production: Heather Kern

Manufactured in the United States of America

October 2002

10 9 8 7 6 5 4 3 2 1

Library of Congress Cataloging-in-Publication Data is available.

ISBN 0-7432-3523-1

ABOUT THE AUTHOR

Chris Kensler majored in English at Indiana University. He has written over a dozen books, covered a presidential campaign for a national news organization, and edited an arts and culture magazine. He is co-founder of the book packager Paper Airplane Projects with his partner, Heather Kern.

ACKNOWLEDGMENTS

The author would like to thank Maureen McMahon for her help shaping and editing the manuscript and Lori DeGeorge for proofreading the book.

TENNESSEE TOLEDO AND HIS

DESERT OF DANGER

It was a hot, sunny day on the Egyptian desert—the kind of day Tennessee Toledo had dreamed of his whole life. He pulled his wide-brimmed hat down over his sweaty forehead and trudged through blowing sand that stung his skin like a million thumbtacks.

"Owwwwwww," moaned Tennessee. "Owwwwwww."

But the pain felt good (like when you scratch a bug bite really hard) because Tennessee was hot on the trail of buried treasure—acres and acres of solid gold french fries, buried with the legendary King Toot in his tomb 5,000 years ago.

Tennessee had spent his last pennies in the Egyptian capital of Cairo to buy the treasure map he held in his sunburned hand. According to the ancient scroll, King Toot's tomb was right below his feet, hidden beneath centuries of sand and dirt.

Tennessee took a drink from his canteen. He had one day's supply of water left. If he didn't find the tomb today, he would have to return to Cairo. He would be the laughingstock of all the successful treasure hunters. They'd call him "rookie" and "junior" and other names he hated even more.

"Just because I'm new at this," he said to himself and put the cap back on his canteen. "It's just not fair."

Suddenly, the stinging wind became a desert tornado! Tennessee fell flat on his belly, as he had learned to do in Desperate Dan's Treasure Hunter Camp. Then, to his horror, he felt himself sinking.

"Holy frijoles!" he screamed and began scrambling out of the sinkhole. But it was too late. Quickly, his body began sinking into the fiery hot quicksand.

"This is my desert of danger!" he cried as the sand came up to his mouth. "Goodbye, cruel wor-!"

The sand covered his head! Tennessee held his breath. He was being sucked down, further and further. The sand grew cooler as he was pulled deeper. Finally he could hold his breath no longer. His last thought before blacking out was of King

> **"Tennessee was hot on the trail of buried treasure—acres and acres of solid gold french fries, buried with King Toot in his tomb 5,000 years ago."**

Toot, the 5,000-year-old boy king.

KING TOOT AND HIS GAUNTLET OF GIANT TOMES

Tennessee woke in darkness. He coughed out a mouthful of sand and checked to make sure all of his limbs were still attached. They were.

"Holy frijoles! Where am I?" he said to himself, still dazed from his ordeal.

"This is my house!" a voice thundered. "And I don't remember inviting anyone over to play!"

The dark room changed from black to ultrabright in an instant. Tennessee rubbed

his eyes. He couldn't believe it. He had found King Toot's tomb!

"My name is Tennessee Toledo," Tennessee called to the air. "Are you the great King Toot? I am searching for King Toot and his Field of Golden Fries!"

The voice was silent. Tennessee stood up and looked around him. He was in a room the size of a football field filled with golden statues, beautiful vases, chests full of scrolls, barrels full of gems, and sarcophaguses full of . . . mummies!

"Holy frijoles!" Tennessee yelled. "King Toot! Are you there?"

One of the caskets began to shake. The

dust of thousands of years slid from its surface as it rose. Tennessee shivered as the door opened and out walked the mummified King Toot.

"I am indeed the Great King Toot!" the mummy bellowed. "And you have invaded my living room! And for that you shall die! But first you must tell me one thing!"

"Holy frijoles!" cried Tennessee. "Please don't kill me! I will tell you what you wish to know."

"What," Toot questioned, "Is a *frijole*? You keep saying *Holy frijoles* this and *Holy frijoles* that. Answer me or die!"

"*Frijole* is the Spanish word for bean," Tennessee explained. "It's pronounced *frih-HOLE-ee*. I just say it because I want it to be my catch phrase when I become a famous treasure hunter and they make a documentary about me on the History Channel."

"Catch phrases . . . Spanish words . . . History Channel," Toot muttered sadly. "I suppose there are a great many things in the world that I know nothing about."

"What do you mean, King Toot?" Tennessee asked.

"I have been buried for 5,000 years, with just my loyal court jester Mel Boinks to talk to, and only a few old books to read,

over and over again," he said. "My jester and I ran out of things to say about 4,000 years ago, and the books are very, very outdated. I am so ashamed!"

With that, the mummy began to sob. No tears came out, because Toot was as dry as a piece of beef jerky under his mummy wrap.

"It's okay, King Toot. I can help you learn about the outside world if you want," Tennessee offered.

"Really?" said King Toot. "Oh, I would be so grateful. I tell you what—let's make a game out of it. If you win the game, you can go free. If you lose the game, you stay here with me forever. Sound like fun?"

"Hmm. Not really," said Tennessee. "How about this? If I win, I get to go free AND I get to take your famous Field of Golden Fries with me."

"You would get my solid gold french fries?" King Toot thought for a moment. "Okay. But only because you will never win. It is impossible make it through my GAUNTLET OF GIANT TOMES!"

Now it was Tennessee who felt like crying.

"There are four rooms in my mummy's tomb," King Toot explained. "Each one of them contains a giant tome: a WORLD ALMANAC, a DICTIONARY, a WORLD ATLAS, and a THESAURUS. The tomes are all very old and outdated!"

"What's a *tome*?" Tennessee asked.

"A *tome* is another word for a *big big big book*," said a voice from another coffin.

"Who's there?" asked the startled explorer.

The lid flew off its casket and out popped a mummy wearing a jester's cap.

"Mel Boinks at your service," said the mummified comedian, offering his hand for Tennessee to shake. Tennessee did, and the jester's hand came off! King Toot roared with laughter.

"Can you give me a hand?" Boinks asked, and King Toot nearly fell over from laughing so hard.

"Boinks, you are as funny as a mummy as you were alive," King Toot said, wiping imaginary tears from his face.

"I'm not sure I like mummy jokes," said Tennessee, returning Boinks' hand.

"Sorry about that," said Boinks. "Gotta keep the king happy. Anyway, it's a pleasure meeting you. We get so few guests! I guess King Toot is explaining his Gauntlet of Giant Tomes already?"

"Yes I am, Boinks, and you have interrupted," said King Toot. "So let me continue. All of my giant tomes have hundreds, if not thousands, of pages in them."

"Holy frijoles!" yelled Tennessee. "Those are big books!"

"Yes, they are," Toot answered. "You will start with my WORLD ALMANAC in Chamber 1. You must add a bunch of information from a modern almanac to my ancient book. Only then will you be allowed to enter the Chamber 2, where you will find my DICTIONARY! If you answer its questions right, you get to work on my WORLD ATLAS. And then on my THESAURUS."

"If you answer my questions

The PalmSpring 7000 has a special feature. You can write notes to Tennessee on this book's special HyperTrans paper, and Tennessee can receive your messages on his PalmSpring 7000!

about these four reference books, you make it through the Gauntlet of Giant Tomes! You get my Field of Golden Fries, and you are free to leave. But if you fail, we will have much more time to get to know each other."

"Let's go grab the good seats in Chamber 1!" yelled Boinks. "I'll bet you ten silver cat statues he doesn't make it past the first chamber!"

"You're on!" said King Toot, and the two ran down a skinny corridor, mummified arm in mummified arm.

Tennessee was worried. He didn't know how he could possibly answer a bunch of questions from King Toot's big, outdated reference books. But wait!

Just before he set off for Egypt, Tennessee's inventor friend Leonard had given him a homemade hand-held computer. Leonard called it his PalmSpring 7000 Personal Digital Assistant. The PalmSpring PDA has a special feature. Leonard can write notes to Tennessee on HyperTrans paper, and Tennessee can receive the notes

on his PalmSpring! Maybe Tennessee could get the answers to King Toot's questions on his PalmSpring 7000!

"Holy frijoles!" Tennessee exclaimed. "This may work. If I can tap out King Toot's questions and get people to write me back on special HyperTrans paper, I may just make it through the Gauntlet of Giant Tomes!"

THIS IS WHERE YOU COME IN

Tennessee needs the readers of this book to find the answers to King Toot's questions in their modern-day WORLD ATLAS, THESAURUS, WORLD ALMANAC, and DICTIONARY!

Secrets of the Giant Tomes Revealed is printed on Leonard's special HyperTrans paper! When you write your answers in the book, the answers are automatically transmitted to Tennessee's PalmSpring 7000! (Don't believe us? Check out the antenna on the back cover.)

If you and the other people who have this book complete all the activities, Tennessee can get all of the information he needs to update King Toot's ancient tomes. With your help, Tennessee can crack the Secrets of the Giant Tomes, find the Field of Golden Fries, and make it back home. Otherwise, Tennessee Toledo is doomed to a life of listening to bad mummy jokes.

DOOMED!

HOW TO USE THIS BOOK

Tennessee Toledo has to make it through four chambers of King Toot's tomb so he can gain his freedom. In each chamber, you need to do a bunch of fun **Inter-Activities** in order to save Tennessee from doom.

For each of these activities, you need a standard, adult version (NOT a kid version) of one of these reference books:

World Almanac   Dictionary
World Atlas   Thesaurus

Most Inter-Activities also have a short **Tome Test** question that leads you into a deeper exploration of your reference book. Other activities have **Tome Tips** to help you learn more about your reference book.

So you will need these reference books by your side to do the Inter-Activities and Tome Tests. Once you complete all of the activities in one chamber, you will be given a final challenge called **King Toot's Hazardous Puzzle of Pain**. It tests all of the skills you learned.

The Hazardous Puzzle of Pain reveals the **Extra Hazardous Password**. If you collect the passwords from all four chambers, you can help Tennessee collect his treasure and escape.

Let's recap. In each chamber you need to:

1 Do the Inter-Activities   **3** Complete the Hazardous Puzzle of Pain

2 Do the Tome Tests and Read the Tome Tips   **4** Collect the Extra Hazardous Password

OKAY, BUT WHAT'S IN IT FOR YOU?

These activities will help you get really good at finding information in a dictionary, almanac, thesaurus, and atlas. Knowing how to use these big books will help you with homework, papers, and tests. Isn't that exciting?.

You can use any good, recently-published reference book to help Tennessee Toledo, but some reference books work a little better than others. Tennessee recommends the following reference books.

WORLD ALMANAC

Use a world almanac published in the last year or two. It is very important that your almanac be new. You don't want an almanac from 1981 because everything that has happened since 1981 won't be in there. Also, make sure your world almanac has the following kinds of information:

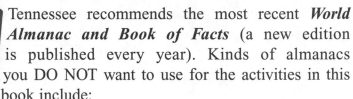

- **Population facts and statistics (world and U.S.)**
- **United States facts and statistics (U.S. presidents, elections, state facts, etc.)**
- **Economic statistics (consumer information, trade statistics, employment statistics, etc.)**
- **History (world history, U.S. history, year in review, etc.)**
- **Sports and awards (Olympics, pro sports, Nobel Prize winners, etc.)**

Tennessee recommends the most recent *World Almanac and Book of Facts* (a new edition is published every year). Kinds of almanacs you DO NOT want to use for the activities in this book include:

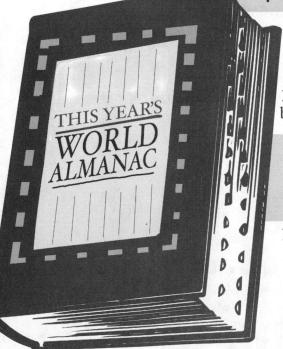

- ***The Farmer's Almanac* (it mostly covers the weather)**
- **Sports almanacs (they cover only sports)**
- **Any world almanac that is more than five years old**

None of these will help you answer the questions in the Gauntlet of Giant Tomes.

Note: The answers to the activities in this book come from the *World Almanac and Book of Facts*.

WORLD ATLAS

Use a full-color world atlas for the activities in this book.
The atlas should have:

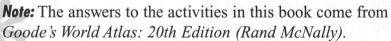

- Maps of all the continents (North America, Asia, etc.)
- Maps of major regions and countries on the continents (United States, Europe, etc.)
- Maps with physical features (mountains, deserts, lakes, etc.)
- Maps with political features (countries, states, cities, etc.)
- Maps with man-made structures (roads, trains, cities, etc.)

Tennessee recommends *Goode's World Atlas: 20th Edition*
and the *Oxford Atlas of the World*. Kinds of atlases you
DO NOT want to use for this book include:

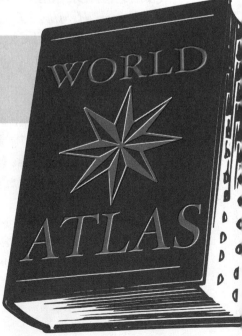

- Road atlases (they just give driving directions)
- Any world atlas that is more than ten years old (country and city
  names and boundaries change, new roads and bridges get built, etc.)

Note: The answers to the activities in this book come from
Goode's World Atlas: 20th Edition (Rand McNally).

DICTIONARY

Use a hardcover version of a college dictionary. Don't worry—just because it's a college edition doesn't mean you have to be in college to use it! College dictionaries just have more information about the words. Pick a dictionary that includes:

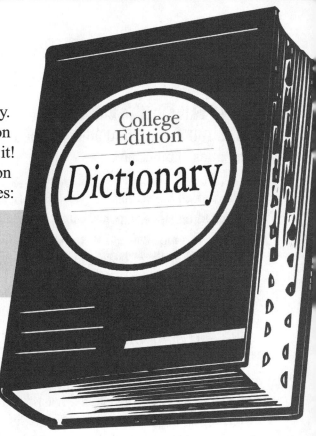

- Pronunciation information
- Etymologies (information about word origins)
- Multiple definitions

Tennessee recommends *Merriam Webster's Collegiate Dictionary: 10th Edition* and *American Heritage Dictionary: Second College Edition*. The kinds of dictionaries you DO NOT want to use for this book include:

- Most pocket/paperback dictionaries (they usually don't have as much information in them because they are smaller)
- Biographical dictionaries (they're good for information about people, but not for words)

Note: The answers to the activities in this book come from *Merriam Webster's Collegiate Dictionary: 10th Edition.*

THESAURUS

Any good English language thesaurus will do nicely for the activities in this book. Tennessee recommends a thesaurus that has:

- An index of word categories (a list of the subjects used to organize the words)
- An index of words

Tennessee recommends **Roget's International Thesaurus: Sixth Edition**. Kinds of thesauri you DO NOT want to use for this book include:

- A really old thesaurus (common synonyms change as the English language changes over the years)

Note: The answers to the activities in this book were found using *Roget's International Thesaurus: Sixth Edition.*

THESAURUS

More than
250,000
WORDS

IF YOU DON'T READ THIS YOU'LL BE SORRY! You can do the Inter-Activities in this book with ANY reference book described on these pages. BUT—and this is a very big BUT—if you use reference books that are different from the ones we recommend, your answers to the Inter-Activities will not match up exactly with the answers in the back of this book. THIS IS NOT A BIG DEAL. The important thing is for you to get to know your reference books, no matter what brand they are. But if you want to be able to check your answers, by all means, use the books we recommend.

Welcome to the first chamber of my Gauntlet of Giant Tomes," King Toot says, seated along with Mel Boinks on a ruby-covered couch in a room made of gold.

In the middle of the chamber, sitting atop a silver pedestal, is King Toot's ancient almanac.

"Nice tomb!" says Tennessee.

"Thanks!" Boinks replies. "I helped decorate it."

Tennessee leafs through the almanac. "It may be old and outdated, but luckily, it's set up just like a modern-day almanac," he notices. "It has a contents page in front, a detailed alphabetical index, and around 1,000 pages of facts and statistics on all sorts of subjects."

"Unfortunately, it is limited to information about ancient Egypt," King Toot replies. "There are about fifty pages on papyrus production; there are only a handful of countries covered in its Nations of the World section; and World History stops, well, when I stopped."

Beware the first chamber of
King Toot's Gauntlet of Giant Tomes!

Chamber 1

You are Here

Chamber 2

Chamber 3

Chamber 4

EXIT!

FOR STARTERS

Take a few minutes
to look through
your almanac.

What are some of
the interesting
subjects it covers?

RESOURCE

World almanac with a
table of contents

SKILL

Using the
table of contents

FACT FINDING 1

Take a look at my almanac's table of contents and tell me if there are any sections that need to be added to it," says King Toot.

Tennessee opens the almanac to its table of contents, which lists the following old and outdated sections:

CONTENTS

"Well," offers Tennessee, "there are probably a few important subjects that could be added to your almanac to make it a bit more complete."

"Then do it already!" yells the impatient boy king. "Just because I enjoy a good mummified handshake joke doesn't mean I'm a nice guy. I was King of Egypt! I expect results!"

Inter-Activity

Tennessee needs you to write down some of the new topics that are covered in the general subjects he has to add to King Toot's old almanac.

1) Use your almanac's table of contents to find the page number for each of the general subjects listed on page 19.

2) Turn to the first page of each general subject section and copy the FIRST topic heading in the space provided. Tennessee has done the first one for you.

Note: The subject names in your almanac may be slightly different than those listed here. For example, your almanac may use "The World's Nations" instead of "Nations of the World." That's okay. Use your common sense. If your almanac doesn't have a section that even comes close to one of the general subjects in this activity, just put an "X" on the line to show that your almanac doesn't cover that information.

First Topic Heading

Aerospace Memorable Moments in Human Spaceflight

Awards and Prizes

Education

Employment

World Exploration and Geography

Health

Historical Figures

Meteorology

Nations of the World (First nation listed)

Sports

State and Local Government

Cities in the U.S. (First city listed)

United States History

Weights and Measures

World History

List 5 subjects in your Table of Contents that are NOT on this list.

1)

2)

3)

4)

5)

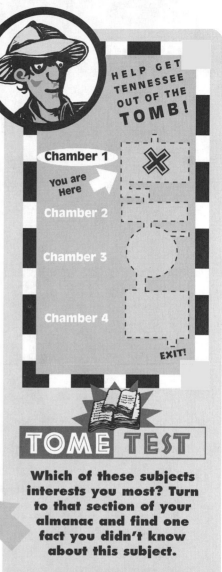

HELP GET TENNESSEE OUT OF THE TOMB!

Chamber 1

You are Here

Chamber 2

Chamber 3

Chamber 4

EXIT!

TOME TEST

Which of these subjects interests you most? Turn to that section of your almanac and find one fact you didn't know about this subject.

Interesting Section:

Interesting Fact:

RESOURCE
World almanac
with an index

SKILL
Using the index

FACT FINDING 2

King Toot is quite pleased with his new table of contents. "The new information you added to my almanac is very helpful," he says. "It should help me shut up my know-it-all royal jester. Ever since he was embalmed so he could keep me company in my afterlife, Mel Boinks has been soooo annoying."

"What do you mean?" asks the shocked jester.

"You keep telling me the same jokes. You keep dropping my expensive vases in your juggling act. And you think you know everything!" King Toot replies.

"Well," Tennessee interrupts, "those subjects I just listed are only the almanac's table of contents—real general stuff. If you really need to know everything that's in an almanac, you need to read the index. That's really detailed."

"Then write me a new index right away," says the impatient boy king.

"You really hurt my feelings this time, King Toot," says Boinks. "I won't forget this as long as I live!" With that, Boinks gets up in a huff and leaves the king alone on his fancy couch.

"Not a problem!" says King Toot. "You're already dead!"

Inter–Activity

Tennessee needs your help filling in the almanac's outdated index. For this activity, you will be using your world almanac's index (also called a *General Index* in many almanacs).

1) Find the first letter of your first name in your almanac's index.

2) Group up to six **bold-faced** headings from that letter of the alphabet under the categories King Toot made up on page 21. (Some categories will have more than six headings, so you will not be able to fit them all.)

3) If you come across something you can't categorize, turn to that page in your almanac and read about it so you can figure it out.

4) List any headings that don't fall under the main categories under "Miscellaneous."

Arts, Entertainment, & Media

_____ _____ _____

_____ _____ _____

Government & Legislation

_____ _____ _____

_____ _____ _____

Places

_____ _____ _____

_____ _____ _____

Buildings & Landmarks

_____ _____ _____

_____ _____ _____

Religion

_____ _____ _____

_____ _____ _____

Weather

_____ _____ _____

_____ _____ _____

Business & Businesses

_____ _____ _____

_____ _____ _____

Science & Technology

_____ _____ _____

_____ _____ _____

People

_____ _____ _____

_____ _____ _____

Sports

_____ _____ _____

_____ _____ _____

Miscellaneous

_____ _____ _____

_____ _____ _____

HELP GET TENNESSEE OUT OF THE TOMB!

Chamber 1

You are Here

Chamber 2

Chamber 3

Chamber 4

EXIT!

TOME TEST

How many different ways of looking things up does your almanac have?

Number of research aids:

_____

List them here, with their page numbers.

_____

_____

_____

READING TABLES 1

I am sorry you had to see me yell at Boinks," says King Toot. "I am sure he will come back soon and I will apologize to him then. He is probably looking at the hieroglyphs of famous Egyptian jesters. That usually makes him feel better."

"Um, okay," says Tennessee.

"And where are you from, my explorer friend?" King Toot asks.

"Tennessee, U.S.A.," he replies. "Like my name."

"Really!" King Toot exclaims. "Tell me more about *Tennessee* and *U.S.A.*"

Visions of corn fields and the Smoky Mountains fill Tennessee's head. He gets homesick.

"I'm too emotional to talk about it right now," he chokes out. "Could I write you a short letter about it instead?"

"Of course my friend," says Toot, pulling off a piece of his mummy wrap so Tennessee can use it to blow his nose.

Inter–Activity

Almanacs are full of tables of information, many of which are organized by state. For this activity, Tennessee needs ONE statistic about your state from FIVE different tables or charts that include your state.

1) Find five statistics about your state.

2) Once you have found five statistics, write King Toot a letter about your home state, using the information given in the tables of statistics.

Note: Here are good ways to find this information:
- Find your state in the index. See what kind of information is provided. Look for statistics on the page numbers listed for your state.
- Turn to subject categories like *population, income,* or *energy* and look for the statistics that mention your state.
- Look up "States, U.S." in your index. Many almanacs have all of the subjects (*population, income,* etc.) listed under this heading. Turn to these page numbers and look for statistics about your state.

State information for your home state of:

_____

1) Section _____
   Statistic _____
2) Section _____
   Statistic _____
3) Section _____
   Statistic _____
4) Section _____
   Statistic _____
5) Section _____
   Statistic _____

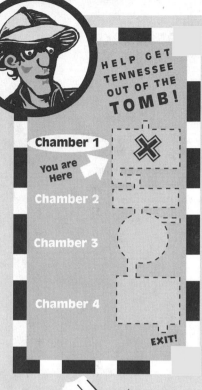

HELP GET TENNESSEE OUT OF THE **TOMB!**

Chamber 1

You are Here

Chamber 2

Chamber 3

Chamber 4

EXIT!

Dear King Toot,

_____
_____
_____
_____
_____
_____
_____
_____
_____
_____
_____

TOME TIP

READING CHARTS
Finding information about your state in a chart is easy if you know where to look. First, pick your chart. Now find your state (Tennessee) or its abbreviation (TN) on the left hand side of the chart. Put a piece of paper or a ruler underneath it, and read all of the information that's printed next to your state.

RESOURCE
World almanac with tables of statistics

SKILL
Converting the figures given in statistics tables into millions, billions, and trillions

READING TABLES 2

King Toot is fascinated by the information about the United States that Tennessee added to his almanac.

"The United States of America sounds like a magical place," says Toot. "Except for the hazardous waste, of course. But I know how that goes—it took us years to figure out how to dispose of disgusting trash."

"Yeah, it's definitely a problem," agrees Tennessee. "With so many people, it's hard to keep everything running smoothly."

"How many people are there now on the planet?" asks Toot.

"Oh, about 6 or 7 billion, give or take a few hundred million."

"B-b-b-billion?" Toot stammers. "I don't believe you!"

"It's true," says Tennessee.

"You're lying!" comes a voice from across the room. Mel Boinks is back! "You're just trying to make my great king feel puny!"

"Am not!" Tennessee yells.

"Are too!" Boinks shoots back.

"Are you?" asks King Toot.

"Not true!" Tennessee replies.

Inter–Activity

Tennessee needs to give King Toot some evidence of just how large the world's population has grown. Almanacs usually abbreviate large numbers to make it easier to fit them into the charts. Tennessee needs you to convert the abbreviated numbers in your almanac back into thousands, millions, billions, and trillions.

1) Fill in the zeros for the big numbers from King Toot's ancient almanac listed on page 25. (Tennessee has done the first one for you.)

2) Find a bunch of real statistics in your almanac.

3) Convert those numbers into thousands, millions, billions, or trillions.

Note: Your almanac may not have some of these figures. If you can't find them, don't worry—do the ones you can and then go straight to the Tome Test.

Common Conversions

Hundreds	100 (2 zeroes)
Thousands	1,000 (3 zeroes)
Millions	1,000,000 (6 zeroes)
Billions	1,000,000,000 (9 zeroes)
Trillions	1,000,000,000,000 (12 zeroes)

HELP GET TENNESSEE OUT OF THE TOMB!

Chamber 1
You are Here
Chamber 2
Chamber 3
Chamber 4
EXIT!

King Toot's Almanac

Mummy Wrap Production
(in *millions* of inches)
2810 B.C.E. 45.2= 45,200,000
2800 B.C.E. 46.3= _____
2790 B.C.E. 52.7= _____

Nile Delta Silt Count
(in *trillions* of grains)
2810 B.C.E. 96.0= 96,000,000,000,000
2800 B.C.E. 112.6= _____
2790 B.C.E. 67.4= _____

Papyrus Production
(in *billions* of scrolls)
2810 B.C.E. 11.3 11,300,000,000
2800 B.C.E. 9.4 _____
2790 B.C.E. 13.5 _____

Invading Hordes
(in *thousands* of soldiers)
2810 B.C.E. 56.3 56,300
2800 B.C.E. 43.2 _____
2790 B.C.E. 145.0 _____

Your World Almanac

National Debt/ Surplus for Year 2000
(*millions* of dollars)

_____

converts to

_____

U.S. Gross Domestic Product (GDP) for Year 2000
(*billions* of dollars)

_____

converts to

_____

U.S. Unemployment for Year 2000
(*thousands* of people)

_____

converts to

_____

TOME TEST

What's the biggest number you can find in your almanac? When you find the number you think is biggest, give your almanac to a friend or family member. Who found the biggest number?

My Big Number

_____

His/Her Big Number

_____

CURRENT EVENTS

I 'm sorry I called you a liar, Tennessee," Boinks apologizes. "It's just that King Toot has never yelled at me like he did, and I took my anger out on you."

"Apology accepted," says Tennessee.

"Good!" says Boinks. "Can I get you anything? A snack? Some raisins? Dried apricots?"

"Sure, thanks," says Tennessee. "I'm starving."

"Boinks is a good jester," King Toot admits after Boinks leaves the chamber. "He is just sensitive. He was one of my most loyal subjects when I was king. But that was long ago, when the world was small. I guess I *was* a puny little king in a puny little world."

"Don't be so hard on yourself, Toot," comforts Tennessee. "Just because things are bigger now doesn't necessarily mean they're better."

"No?" King Toot says, brightening. "You mean that the world was a better place when I was its leader?"

"Well, I don't know about better," Tennessee says. "Just . . . different."

"I need concrete examples Tennessee!" yells the impatient boy king. "I need to know some of the things that are going on now in the world. Good or bad—I must know!"

Inter-Activity

Tennessee needs you to provide King Toot with short summaries of some recent events.

1) Go to your almanac's "Year in Review" section and find the chronology of the year's events. That's the list of things that happened in the year your almanac was being written.

2) Write down, in chronological order, the birthdays of five family members or friends, along with their names.

3) Under each name and date, write down one or two entries from your current events section that happened on or around that birthday.

Birthday #1 _____ **Who** _____

Current Event: _____

_____

_____

_____

Birthday #2 _____ **Who** _____

Current Event: _____

_____

_____

_____

_____

Birthday #3 _____ **Who** _____

Current Event: _____

_____

_____

_____

_____

Birthday #4 _____ **Who** _____

Current Event: _____

_____

_____

_____

_____

Birthday #5 _____ **Who** _____

Current Event: _____

_____

_____

_____

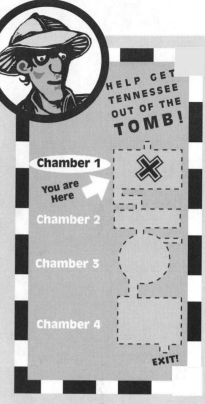

HELP GET
TENNESSEE
OUT OF THE
TOMB!

Chamber 1

You are
Here

Chamber 2

Chamber 3

Chamber 4

EXIT!

TOME TEST

Go to your almanac's "Year in Review" section and find an event that happened on or around YOUR birthday. Write it down here:

_____

_____

_____

_____

Do you remember this happening? Yes ❏ No ❏

U.S. GOVERNMENT

"From what you have shown me, I think the world *was* a better place 5,000 years ago," says King Toot. "Don't you think so, Boinks?"

Mel Boinks returns, eating a handful of golden raisins. He offers some raisins to Tennessee, who takes a handful.

"Whatever," says Boinks, and stuffs the rest of the raisins into the mouth hole in his mummy wrap.

"None for me?" the annoyed boy asks in horror. "When I was ruler of Egypt, you would have been beheaded for being so selfish!"

"Behead me then!" yells Boinks. "Oh wait, it wouldn't matter, because I'm *already dead*. Because you *mummified me* so you would have someone to keep you company in the *afterworld*."

"I will bet the king of the U.S.A. never had to put up with ungrateful jesters like Boinks," says Toot.

"Actually, there is no king of the U.S.A.," corrects Tennessee. "We have a democracy where we elect a president every four years to run things."

Inter-Activity

King Toot wants to know about some recent presidents and the people who worked in their administrations.

Fill in the names of the people who held the following positions in:

1) The current president's administration

2) President John F. Kennedy's administration

3) The administration of the president who was serving when you were born

Note: Most world almanacs have a section on the U.S. government, presidents of the United States, and presidential elections. These are all good places to look for the information to complete this exercise.

The Administration of the Current President

Year: _____ President: _____

His Staff

Vice president _____

Secretary of state _____

Secretary of defense _____

Secretary of treasury _____

Attorney general _____

The Administration of John F. Kennedy

Year: 1960

His Staff

Vice president _____

Secretary of state _____

Secretary of defense _____

Secretary of treasury _____

Attorney general _____

The Administration of the Year You Were Born

Year: _____ President: _____

His Staff

Vice president _____

Secretary of state _____

Secretary of defense _____

Secretary of treasury _____

Attorney general _____

HELP GET TENNESSEE OUT OF THE **TOMB!**

Chamber 1

You are Here

Chamber 2

Chamber 3

Chamber 4

EXIT!

TOME TEST

The president's staff is called his *cabinet*. The five cabinet members listed in this exercise are the most important ones, but there are lots of other cabinet positions. Find three more cabinet positions in your almanac:

1. _____

2. _____

3. _____

RESOURCE

World almanac with presidential voting records and congressional membership lists

SKILL

Finding information in your almanac

ELECTIONS

King Toot is still confused about the United States government. "So many kings of the U.S.A. in so little time!" Toot exclaims. "Your country must be at constant war."

"You aren't listening," says Tennessee. "We don't have kings. We have regular elections where the people pick the president and other representatives."

"You mean being king of the U.S.A. is not a divine right?" the startled Toot asks.

"No—we all have the right to life, liberty, and the pursuit of happiness," explains Tennessee. "Everyone has those, not just the president."

"Can you believe this, Boinks?" Toot asks his jester.

"You bet, Tooters," mutters Boinks. "A lot of folks in Egypt wanted to get you out of power. Including me! Voting sounds like a great invention."

Inter-Activity

Help Tennessee find information about your state's current members of Congress and information about which presidential candidate your state picked in the 2000 election.

1) Look up the names of the senators and members of the House of Representatives from your state, and find out which party each one represents. Write down:

D for Democrat
G for Green party
I for Independent
R for Republican

Good places to start include:
- The section about the current U.S. Congress
- The section covering state and local governments
- The index entry about your state

2) Fill in the information about the most recent presidential election.

Note: The number or representatives for your state is based on your state's population. Some states have only two representatives, while California has more that fifty. If you live in a big state, write down as many representatives as you can fit on these lines.

HELP GET TENNESSEE OUT OF THE TOMB!

Chamber 1

You are Here

Chamber 2

Chamber 3

Chamber 4

EXIT!

Your State: _____

Your State's Congressional Representation

Senate	Party
1. _____	
2. _____	

House of Representatives Party

_____

_____

_____

_____

_____

_____

_____

_____

_____

_____

Your State's Presidential Voting Record Year: 2000 (Top 4)

Candidate	Vote Total
1.	_____
2.	_____
3.	_____
4.	_____

What party did the winner represent?

_____

Did he end up winning the general election? Yes ❑ No ❑

Who came in third in your state?

_____

Which party did he represent?

_____

Who came in last?

_____

Which party did he represent?

_____

Who would you have voted for?

_____

TOME TEST

Which candidate LOST each of the following presidential elections? Circle your answer.

Year	Candidates	
2000	Bush	Gore
1992	Bush	Clinton
1980	Reagan	Carter
1960	Nixon	Kennedy
1948	Dewey	Truman
1912	Wilson	Roosevelt
1880	Garfield	Hancock
1844	Clay	Polk
1828	Adams	Jackson
1796	Adams	Jefferson

RESOURCE

World almanac with facts on U.S. pollution and energy production

SKILL

Finding information; labeling a map

THE ENVIRONMENT

B oinks!" commands King Toot, "Never call me Tooters again! I have had enough of you! Go get us some iced tea!"

"Is it me, or is it hot in here?" the boy king asks Tennessee. "It could be my layers of mummy wrap, but over the last decade or two, I've noticed that this tomb gets uncomfortably hot in the afternoon."

"I am a little warm," Tennessee admits. "It's probably getting hotter in here because of global warming."

"What does that mean, *global warming*?"

"Here's your stupid tea," says Boinks, offering each a tall, cool vase.

"Thanks Boinks," says Tennessee. "All of the fuel-burning vehicles and factories we have built in the past century have created tons of pollution, you see, and that pollution is trapping the heat on the planet that used to get bounced back up into the atmosphere. It could really mess up the environment if we don't do something about it."

"I do not understand the following words," says Toot. "*Pollution—fuel—vehicles—factories—atmosphere—environment*. You must explain."

Inter–Activity

Tennessee has a lot of explaining to do. Help him by identifying some environmental problem spots on this map of the United States.

Most almanacs have information about pollution levels in different cities. You can also find information about pollution in sections covering the search for energy resources and energy production. Information on the following subjects should help you fill in your map:

- Big coal mines
- Nuclear accidents
- Large oil fields
- Toxic chemical releases
- Poor air quality
- Hazardous waste sites

1) Try to find at least five places where the environment may be in danger.

2) Label the map with the name of each place with an environmental problem.

HELP GET TENNESSEE OUT OF THE TOMB!

Chamber 1

You are Here

Chamber 2

Chamber 3

Chamber 4

EXIT!

Place #1

Description of problem

Place #2

Description of problem

Place #3

Description of problem

Place #4

Description of problem

Place #5

Description of problem

TOME TEST

Does your almanac have a list of endangered animals? Find it and list three groups of animals here, along with how many animals from each group are endangered in the U.S.

Species	Number
1.	
2.	
3.	

RESOURCE

World almanac with
U.S. census figures

SKILL

Graphing and
comparing statistics
over time

POPULATIONS

"So let me get this straight," says King Toot. "There are billions of people on the planet now, and all of these people cause a lot of pollution."

"That's right," says Tennessee, sipping his drink. "Especially in the United States. We aren't the biggest country in the world, but we use the most energy, which means we cause the most pollution."

"How many people live in the United States?" asks Toot.

"Oh, about 270 or 280 million," Tennessee explains. "China and India are much, much larger. They both have more than a billion people each."

"Tell me more about your states," says Toot. "Are they all the same size?"

"No, they are different shapes and sizes," says Tennessee. "Some states don't even have a million people in them, but others, like California and New York, have tens of millions of people."

"King Toot lived in a state all by himself," Boinks interrupts. "A state of confusion!"

Inter–Activity

For this activity you are going to make line graphs that show the population growth of three states. King Toot wants to know about three states in particular: one from the East (Connecticut), one from the Midwest (Indiana) and one from the West (Nevada).

1) Turn to the U.S. Population section of your almanac.

2) Find the table that charts the populations of the U.S. states over time.

3) Fill in the populations for the years that Tennessee needs information for. (Indiana is already done.)

4) Plot those years on the graph. Use a different kind of line for each state—a continuous line for Connecticut and a dashed line for Nevada. (Indiana is already done.)

Note: These three states were admitted to the union at different times, so each line you draw will have a different starting year.

Find the population for each state listed below for the following years. Tennessee has done Indiana for you.

POPULATIONS LIST

	CT	IN	NV
1790		--	
1800		6	
1850		988,416	
1860		1,350,428	
1900		2,516,462	
1910		2,700,816	
1950		3,934,224	
1960		4,662,498	
2000		6,080,48	

KEY
CT ———
IN ········
NV ------

Plot the populations you just found on this graph. Tennessee has done Indiana for you.

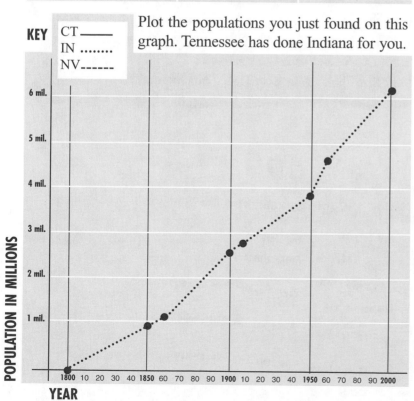

POPULATION IN MILLIONS

YEAR

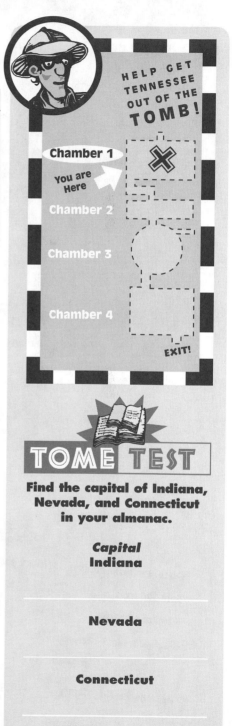

HELP GET TENNESSEE OUT OF THE TOMB!

Chamber 1
You are Here
Chamber 2
Chamber 3
Chamber 4
EXIT!

TOME TEST

Find the capital of Indiana, Nevada, and Connecticut in your almanac.

Capital
Indiana

_____

Nevada

_____

Connecticut

_____

WORLD ALMANAC

U.S. FACTS

Boinks!" screams King Toot. "I have had enough of your insults! Plus there is a dead fly in my iced tea!"

"That's your fingertip!" screeches Boinks. "You really should be more careful!"

"Drat!" says Toot. "Sometimes being a mummy is disgusting."

"So what was ancient Egypt like when you guys were around?" asks Tennessee. "I've studied hundreds of books about it, but I'd love to hear about it from some mummies who were actually there."

"Egypt was the land of kings," sighs Toot. "I was beloved by the people, all of whom were rich and healthy. We had more gold than you can imagine, and traders from across the world came to us and paid thousands of cowrie shells for our products."

"Blah blah blah blah blah," says Boinks. "Some of that's true, but not all of it. Here, let me write about it in the sand with some statistics I pulled out of Tooter's almanac."

"I am *King Toot*!" yells King Toot. "*Not* Tooters!"

Egypt 2800 BCE

Gross Domestic Product . . 5,700.2 thousand cowrie shells

Gold Reserves . . . . 183 troy ounces

Number of Farms 987,000

Foreign Trade: . . . Imports   456.2 thousand cowrie shells

Exports   872.9 thousand cowrie shells

Average Teacher Salary . . . . 4 goats and 10 chickens

Most Popular Newspaper . . . . Egypt Today

Daily Circulation 16

Top Rated Entertainment . . . . The Mel Boinks Comedy Hour

Most Popular Boy Name . . . . Imanhotep

Most Popular Girl Name . . . . Isis

Average Life Expectancy 19

Inter-Activity

Tennessee needs to give Toot ten statistics about the United States to match those used by Mel Boinks in his overview of life in ancient Egypt.

1) Find ten statistics about the United States for the categories below. Write them down along with the almanac section where you found the statistic.

United States 2000

Category	Statistic	Section
Gross domestic product (GDP)		
Gold reserves		
Number of farms		
Foreign trade:		
Imports		
Exports		
Average teacher salary		
Most popular newspaper		
Daily circulation		
Top rated TV show (2000-2001)		
Most popular boy name		
Most popular girl name		
Average life expectancy		

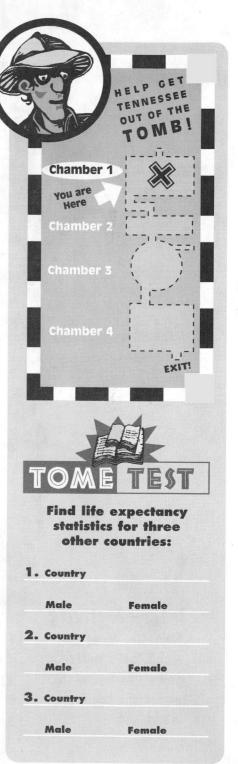

HELP GET TENNESSEE OUT OF THE TOMB!

Chamber 1

You are Here

Chamber 2

Chamber 3

Chamber 4

EXIT!

TOME TEST

Find life expectancy statistics for three other countries:

1. Country _____

Male _____ **Female** _____

2. Country _____

Male _____ **Female** _____

3. Country _____

Male _____ **Female** _____

WORLD LEADERS

"Ancient Egypt was a great place to be king," King Toot continues. "But it wasn't always easy. Every day I had people coming from miles away to give me gifts. There were so many people visiting, I had a hard time keeping their names straight."

"Oh that sounds *so rough*," Boinks says sarcastically.

"Don't interrupt," growls the boy king. "Anyway, I had a special trick I used to keep everyone's name straight. It was taught to me by my dear mother, Queen Tootsie. As I was introduced to each admirer, I would combine a letter from his name into my own, like so."

Leader	Area of Rule
KING GINSENG	Upper Tiber
FRITZ THE GREAT	Fertile Crescent
MOMO THE INSIPID	Third Hill on the Left
FANG	Desert of Fire
CAMISOLE FLATFOOT	Point of No Return
BILLY IDOLT	Papyrus Fields
QUEEN ODDITY	Memphis
TOOTHLESS PHRANK	Port of Call

"So every day, I would learn the names of a bunch of admirers, and every night, at my admirers' banquet, I would repeat all of their names," he explains. "See how hard it can be to be king!"

Inter-Activity

Tennessee needs you to match Toot's mental powers by finding the names of a bunch of world leaders.

1) Write your first or last name vertically down the page. (Use the longest of your two names.)

2) Find leaders from foreign countries whose names include a letter in your name, and write them down like King Toot did above.

3) After you create your list, close the book and try to recite the list of leaders you created.

Your Name

Leader																				
Leader																				
Leader																				
Leader																				
Leader																				
Leader																				
Leader																				
Leader																				
Leader																				
Leader																				
Leader																				
Leader																				
Leader																				
Leader																				
Leader																				
Leader																				
Leader																				
Leader																				
Leader																				
Leader																				

Country

_____
_____
_____
_____
_____
_____
_____
_____
_____
_____
_____
_____
_____
_____
_____
_____
_____
_____
_____
_____

TOME TEST

Pick the country from your list you know the least about. Look up the following information:

Country _____

Population _____

Location _____

Principle language(s) _____

_____

Monetary unit _____

HELP GET
TENNESSEE
OUT OF THE
TOMB!

Chamber 1

You are
Here

Chamber 2

Chamber 3

Chamber 4

EXIT!

RESOURCE

World almanac with summer and winter Olympics results

SKILL

Researching one section of the almanac

SPORTS FACTS

"Of course I did not spend all of my time getting presents," sighs King Toot. "No, there were always plenty of leisure activities for a boy king who just wanted to have fun. Sports, I think you call them?"

"Oh yeah?" says Tennessee. "Like tennis and soccer?"

"No," explains Toot. "Like Bean Turtle, the sport of kings."

"Toot was the best Bean Turtler around," Boinks admits. "I'll give him that."

"What is Bean Turtle?" asks Tennessee.

"You start with ten big box turtles and ten little bean bags," explains King Toot. "The referee releases the big box turtles and two players each try to toss their little bean bags onto the turtles' backs. The player who gets the most bags on the backs wins."

"Then what?" asks Tennessee.

"Bean Turtle is a tournament sport, so in each round, some players are eliminated," the king continues. "In the second round, the first-round winners square off with twenty turtles, and so on, until the final round, when there are just two players left, and a hundred turtles are set free! The winner of the final round is the Bean Turtle champion, and the loser has to get all the turtles back in their pen!"

"It's quite exciting!" Boinks says sarcastically.

Inter-Activity

King Toot's almanac only lists Egypt's Bean Turtle champions. Tennessee needs you to fill in the following Olympic champions in a variety of summer and winter sports. Use your world almanac's sports section to find the gold medalists in these sports.

WINTER OLYMPICS

Downhill: Men's
1984 Gold Medal
Athlete: _____
Country: _____

Figure Skating: Pairs
1924 Gold Medal
Athlete: _____
Country: _____

Figure Skating: Women's
1998 Gold Medal
Athlete: _____
Country: _____

Speed Skating: Women's 500 Meters
1968 Gold Medal
Athlete: _____
Country: _____

Speed Skating: Men's 1,500 Meters
1988 Gold Medal
Athlete: _____
Country: _____

Snowboarding: Men's Halfpipe
1998 Gold Medal
Athlete: _____
Country: _____

SUMMER OLYMPICS

100-Meter Run: Women's
2000 Gold Medal
Athlete: _____
Country: _____

50-Kilometer Walk: Men's
1984 Gold Medal
Athlete: _____
Country: _____

Discus Throw: Women's
1992 Gold Medal
Athlete: _____
Country: _____

100-Meter Backstroke: Men's
1988 Gold Medal
Athlete _____
Country: _____

100-Meter Butterfly: Women's
1968 Gold Medal
Athlete: _____
Country: _____

Platform Diving: Women's
1996 Gold Medal
Athlete: _____
Country: _____

Middleweight Boxing: Men's
1976 Gold Medal
Athlete: _____
Country: _____

HELP GET TENNESSEE OUT OF THE TOMB!

Chamber 1
You are Here
Chamber 2
Chamber 3
Chamber 4
EXIT!

Which of the countries represented by medal-winners in this activity no longer exist?

_____
_____

Where can you find information about what happened to them in your almanac?

_____
_____

RESOURCE

World almanac listing winners of Nobel, Pulitzer, and other prizes

SKILL

Compiling information by year

AWARDS AND PRIZES

King Toot's constant bragging is wearing on Tennessee. When the king and Boinks leave to find dried lemons for their tea, Tennessee grabs the opportunity to take a nap.

Seconds after his eyes shut, Tennessee is lost in a dream world—the world he will see when he escapes from King Toot's tomb.

There he is, on a large stage in front of tens of thousands of people. They are cheering his name: *Ten-nes-see, Ten-nes-see.* He is wearing a tuxedo and his floppy explorer's hat. A beautiful blonde fashion model comes out from behind the stage's curtain. She is holding a gold statue.

"For he's a jolly good fellow," she chirps, approaching him. "For he's a jolly good fellow." Now the whole crowd is singing with her.

"For he's a jolly good fellow! That nobody can deny!"

A group of famous explorers parades across the stage. Tennessee recognizes Daniel Boone, Sir Francis Drake, and Ernest Shackleton—his heroes! Shackleton steps forward.

"We, the greatest explorers ever, are humbled by your great achievement," he says. "So, in recognition of your outstanding discovery of King Toot's Field of Golden Fries, I present to you the Nobel Peace Prize!"

The crowd applauds. The blonde fashion model kisses him on the cheek. Tennessee takes the prize, and is about to make a speech when Boinks wakes him up.

"You were muttering about something called the Nobel Peace Prize," says Boinks. "The king needs to know what that means."

Inter–Activity

King Toot needs to fill his almanac with award winners. Find the winners of the following awards from the year you were born. Most almanacs have a section listing the winners of various awards. You can also find them by looking in your index under the name of each award.

Year you were born:

_____

	Award Winner
Nobel Prize in Medicine	
Nobel Peace Prize	
Pulitzer Prize in Fiction	
Pulitzer Prize in Poetry	
Newberry Medal	
Miss America	
Academy Award: Best Picture	
Academy Award: Best Actress	
Grammy Award: Album of the Year	
Grammy Award: Song of the Year	

Who would YOU give the following prizes to TODAY:

Nobel Peace Prize

Academy Award: Best Picture

Newberry Medal

Grammy Award: Song of the Year

Miss America

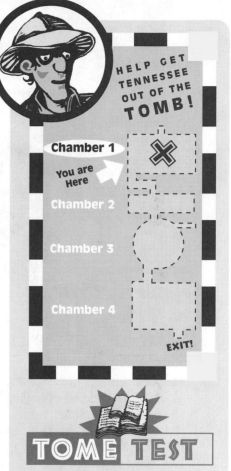

HELP GET TENNESSEE OUT OF THE TOMB!

Chamber 1

You are Here

Chamber 2

Chamber 3

Chamber 4

EXIT!

TOME TEST

How many of the last ten winners of the following awards have you even heard of?

Grammy Award: Record of the Year

Academy Award: Best Actor

Caldecott Medal Books

RESOURCE

A world almanac

SKILL

Using the whole almanac

KING TOOT'S HAZARDOUS PUZZLE OF PAIN

1

I am very impressed with your knowledge, Tennessee," says King Toot. "Now you must pass one more test to make it to my next tome chamber. This test is the hardest one of all!"

"I've got ten silver cat statues riding on this," Boinks tells Tennessee. "If you lose, I win!"

"Shut up Boinks!" yells King Toot. "Now concentrate, Tennessee. Concentrate."

Inter–Activity

King Toot's Hazardous Puzzle of Pain looks like an ordinary crossword puzzle, but it is sooo difficult, it has driven dozens of explorers mad. Use your world almanac to answer the questions, then proceed to the Extra Hazardous Password Question.

ACROSS

1 - 2000 World Series MVP (baseball player)
6 - most populous U.S. state
8 - 17th U.S. state to become a state
10 - 1952 NL pennant winner (_____, New York)
12 - capital of Albania
14 - winner of 1960 Nobel Prize for Literature
16 - Trent _____, Republican senator from Mississippi
17 - nation with the largest active duty armed forces
18 - first word of the U.S. Constitution
20 - 2000 Summer Olympics gold-medal winner in men's soccer
24 - common name for an atlas's meteorological section
26 - alphabetical listing of almanac's contents
27 - acronym for the World Trade Organization
29 - Confederate general defeated by Grant in the Civil War's Battle of Appomatox
30 - largest Great Lake

DOWN

1 - winner of the Academy Award for Best Actress, 1978, _____ Fonda (first name)

2 - East Indies island with an area of 13,094 square miles
3 - 37th U.S. president
4 - _____ Britain (also, _____ wall of China)
5 - 40th president of the U.S.
6 - second largest U.S. county by population
7 - U.S. city with the busiest airport (also the host city of the 1996 Olympic Summer Games)
9 - 1994 National Basketball Association champion (city)
10 - 1988 British Open champion (golf)
11 - ruling family in England in the late 1400s (also the namesake of the U.S.'s largest city)
13 - abbreviation for Idaho
15 - President Hayes' vice president
19 - highest mountain in the U.S.
21 - President John F. Kennedy's assassin
22 - state served by the telephone area code 512
23 - 2000 Olympics gold medal winner, women's 200 meter run
25 - Supreme Court judge who served 1921-30
28 - 1992 Olympics gold medal winner, men's nordic combined skiing

EXTRA HAZARDOUS PASSWORD QUESTION

What do the letters from squares A, B, and C spell?

Password 1

___ ___ ___
A   B   C

CHAMBER 2

"I think there's a certain royal jester who owes me ten silver cat statues," King Toot gloats.

"Thanks a lot, Tennessee," mopes Boinks. "Now I have to go lug a bunch of heavy metal cats out of the treasure pile."

"My world almanac is perfect!" King Toot continues. "But now I need you to fix my dusty old dictionary."

The happy boy king leads Tennessee on hands and knees through a stone tunnel to the second tome chamber. King Toot's Royal Dictionary sits on a stone pedestal.

Tennessee opens it. The dictionary has a bunch of information in front and about 1,500 pages of definitions. Tennessee is glad the definitions are in English and not hieroglyphs!

"How did you know English back then?" he asks the king.

"I didn't," says Toot. "I have a confession to make. You are not the first explorer to fall into my tomb. The last one translated my hieroglyphs into English."

"Wow!" exclaims Tennessee. "Where is he now?"

Toot motions to a pile of bones propped up against the wall of Chamber 2.

Uh oh.

DICTIONARY

Fear the second chamber of
King Toot's Gauntlet of Giant Tomes!

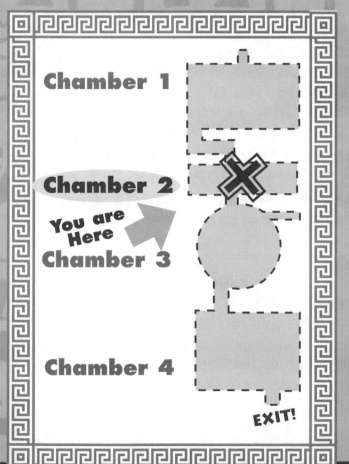

Chamber 1

Chamber 2

You are Here

Chamber 3

Chamber 4

EXIT!

FOR STARTERS

Take a few minutes
to look through your
dictionary. Are any
parts of it confusing?
If so, ask a teacher
or librarian to explain
how to use them.

DICTIONARY

RESOURCE
English language
dictionary

SKILL
Understanding
common dictionary
abbreviations

ABBREVIATIONS

D o not worry about that pile of bones. You are much smarter than he was," reassures Toot. "You are one frukish grinka."

"Thanks—I guess," says a nervous Tennessee. He approaches the dictionary sitting on top of the pedestal.

"Now that I know more about the modern world, I need to be able to talk and loton about it," King Toot explains. "And to be able to loton about it well, I am going to need a really, really good dictionary. Unfortunately, my dictionary is worse than a pile of zerbits."

"A pile of what?" asks Tennessee.

"You know, zerbits," says Toot. "The bits of gunk left over after a thorough toe and fingernail cleaning."

Tennessee freezes. He doesn't understand much of Toot's language. How can he get out of the dictionary chamber not knowing what the heck Toot is talking about? Tennessee needs to get comfortable with the weird words in King Toot's vocabulary.

Inter–Activity

Tennessee looks up the four strange words King Toot just used: *frukish, grinka, loton,* and *zerbits.* The definitions are full of the abbreviations that modern dictionaries use to explain what words mean and how they are pronounced.

1) Find your dictionary's list of abbreviations and guide to pronunciation. These are usually found either at the front of the book before the definitions, or at the back.

2) Answer the questions on the next page about the definitions from King Toot's ancient dictionary.

fruk·ish /'frük-ish/ *adj* 1. Intelligent or smart. 2. Pertaining to or characteristic of a fruk. 3. *Naut* With the wind. **–fruk'ish·ly** *adv* **fruk'ish·ness** *n*

lo·ton /lō-'tən/ *vb* **–toned, –toning, –tones.** [Fr *lotoner*, to emote.] 1. To write with emotion. 2. *Dram* To portray with great feeling. *–tr n* **–ton.** 1. An emotional writer. 2. A crybaby.

grin·ka /grin-'kə /*n pl* **grinkae**. [Lat *grinkus*, to smile.] 1. Handsome fellow. 2. Table with a smooth finish. 3. *Biol* Ideal mate for an organism.

zer·bit /'zər-bit/ [Gk *zerbitos*, remainder.] *n* 1. A leftover. 2. *Chem* An accumulation left as a result of a chemical reaction. 3. *Math.* Remainder left after long division. 4. *Informal.* The gunk beneath a toenail or fingernail.

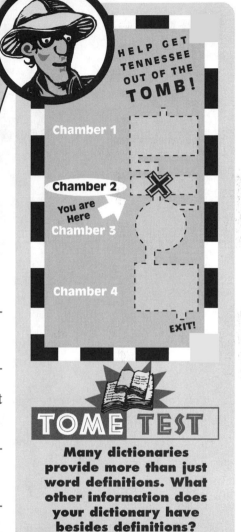

HELP GET TENNESSEE OUT OF THE TOMB!

Chamber 1

Chamber 2
You are Here
Chamber 3

Chamber 4

EXIT!

TOME TEST

Many dictionaries provide more than just word definitions. What other information does your dictionary have besides definitions?

My Dictionary's Other Sections

1. Which definition of *frukish* applies to sailing?

_____

2. What part of speech is *frukishly*?

_____

3. How is the first "o" in *loton* pronounced? How about the second "o"?

_____

4. What is the Latin root of *grinka*?

_____

5. Which definition of *grinka* is King Toot probably using when referring to Tennessee?

_____

6. What do the abbreviations in definitions 2 and 3 of *zerbit* mean?

_____

7. What language does *loton* come from?

_____

DICTIONARY

SYLLABLES AND PRONUNCIATION

"**H**oly frijoles!" exclaims Tennessee. "That was fun learning all your weird words!"

"Well, it was not as much fun as Bean Turtle," King Toot says. "But you are right, it was note halif bade."

"What did you say?" Tennessee asks. "*Note halif bade?*"

"Yes, that is what I said," Toot grumbles. "Do you not understand your own language? I said it was *note halif bade!* That means it was pretty good! Are you making fun of me? I do not have to let you out of here, you know!"

"Calm down, calm down—I think I've figured out what you're saying," says Tennessee. "*Not half bad*. That's what you mean, right? *Not half bad* means *pretty good.*"

"I am so ashamed," moans the embarrassed boy king. "I cannot even pronounce the simplest of English words! I meant *not half bad* but I said *note halif bade*. What am I going to do?"

"Luckily, modern dictionaries give you the pronunciation of the word, along with the definition," says Tennessee.

"Then I know what your next test is," laughs King Toot, very pleased with himself. "And you had better do *pretty good!*"

"You mean *pretty well*," corrects Tennessee.

"What?" the angry boy king asks through gritting teeth.

"Nothing," Tennessee says, turning back to the dictionary.

Inter–Activity

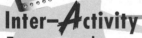

Tennessee needs your help teaching King Toot how to pronounce a bunch of words.

1) Say aloud each of the words on the next page.

2) Break each word into syllables and write down how you think the word is pronounced. Write the syllable or syllables that get stressed in CAPITAL LETTERS. (Tennessee has done the first one for you.)

3) Look up each word and copy the dictionary's pronunciation. Compare your version of the word's pronunciation to your dictionary's.

	Your Pronunciation	Dictionary Pronunciation
cello	CHEL-low	'che-(,)lō
oblige		
groggy		
papaya		
igneous		
rambunctious		
ancient		
leader		
uranium		
scheme		
migraine		
telemetry		
nuclear		
vocabulary		
beret		

HELP GET
TENNESSEE
OUT OF THE
TOMB!

Chamber 1

Chamber 2
You are Here
Chamber 3

Chamber 4

EXIT!

TOME TEST

**Pick three words you
would use to describe
yourself. Copy down your
dictionary's pronunciation
for each word.**

1.

pronunciation

2.

pronunciation

3.

pronunciation

DICTIONARY

RESOURCE
English language
dictionary

SKILL
Identifying parts
of speech

PARTS OF SPEECH

"Where did my jester go?" King Toot says to the room. "This dictionary fixing is getting serious. I need a good laugh!"

"The last time I saw him, he was going to get you the silver cats you won in your bet," Tennessee replies. "He said something about looking in your treasure pile."

"The treasure pile!" yells the surprised boy king. "I forgot to tell him that I surrounded the treasure pile with flesh-eating bats!"

King Toot runs off to find what is left of Mel Boinks, and Tennessee Toledo has a moment to catch his breath. Thanks to your answers, he is doing great in King Toot's Gauntlet of Tomes, but the pressure is starting to get to him.

"I miss my friends," he sighs. "I wonder what Georgia and Leonard are up to right now? Leonard is probably inventing computer hardware, and Georgia is probably studying."

Tennessee really, really misses his girlfriend Georgia. King Toot has had him so busy he hasn't had a chance to contact her and let her know he's okay. When he didn't return to Cairo, the other explorers probably thought the worst!

Tennessee taps out a love letter to her on his PalmSpring 7000, just so Georgia knows he's okay, and that he misses her.

Inter–Activity

Tennessee needs you to find the parts of speech for a bunch of words in his love letter to Georgia. He'll add the parts of speech to King Toot's dictionary.

1) Using your dictionary, make a list of all the different parts of speech each **bold-faced** word in Tennessee's letter could be.

2) For each word, circle the actual part of speech it represents in Tennessee's letter.

Dearest Georgia,

How do I **love** thee? Let me count the ways. While I may be far **from** home, trapped in the tomb of an old mummy, I never **tire** of thinking of you. How are things? Have you heard **back** from the **school** you applied to yet? I do hope you get in. If you don't, well, that's just not **fair**! Laser Dermatology Tech would be lucky to have a woman of your **caliber**.

But I am avoiding the **point**. The point is I **miss** you, **and** I may never see you again! King Toot is making me **pass** a series of tests. If I succeed, I will be rich. **Hey!** I'll buy you your own laser dermatology school! If I fail, I will be trapped in this tomb forever, and will likely die of starvation, unless I develop a **taste** for dried **skin**.

Please pray for me! I love love love you.

Yours forever, **Tennessee**

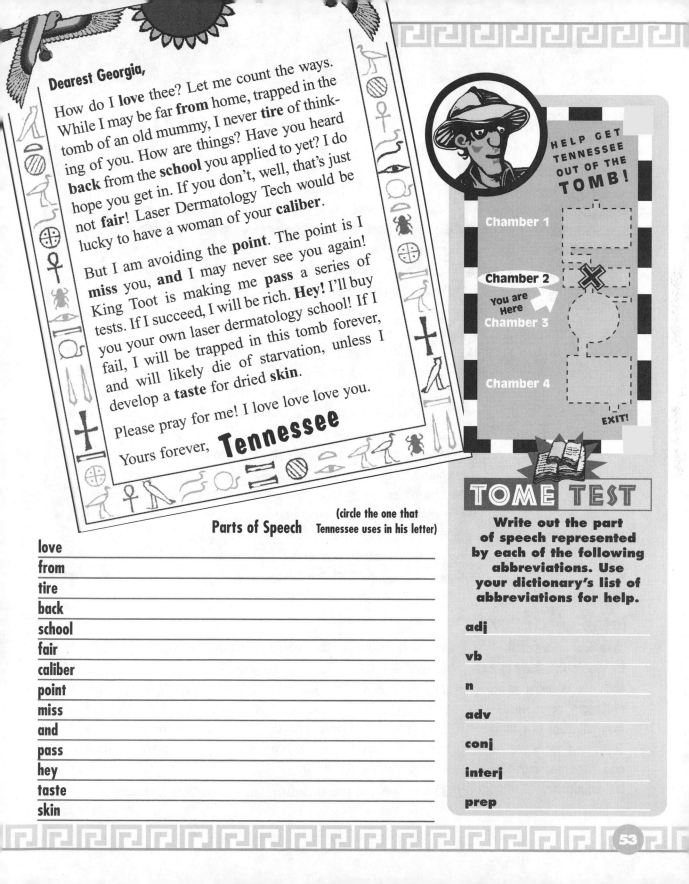

HELP GET TENNESSEE OUT OF THE TOMB!

Chamber 1

Chamber 2

You are Here

Chamber 3

Chamber 4

EXIT!

Parts of Speech
(circle the one that Tennessee uses in his letter)

love _____
from _____
tire _____
back _____
school _____
fair _____
caliber _____
point _____
miss _____
and _____
pass _____
hey _____
taste _____
skin _____

TOME TEST

Write out the part of speech represented by each of the following abbreviations. Use your dictionary's list of abbreviations for help.

adj _____

vb _____

n _____

adv _____

conj _____

interj _____

prep _____

DICTIONARY

MULTIPLE MEANINGS

King Toot returns from the treasure pile with a bat-pecked Boinks.

"Are you okay?" Tennessee asks. Boinks' jester's cap is destroyed, and there are gaping holes in his mummy wrap.

"Does it look like I'm okay?" Boinks replies. "I'm a mess! It's going to take me hours to sew everything back up. And one of the flesh-eating bats flew off with my funny bone!"

"What? I'm sorry, I wasn't listening there for a second," says Tennessee, yawning. "I'm tired."

"Nothing!" screams Boinks, and storms off.

"I'm sorry I upset Boinks," Tennessee says to King Toot, "but I'm beat. I feel like I've been beating my head against a wall trying to figure out your old books. It's like I'm a cop, walking the same beat night after night. I think I need to take a couple of beats and just relax. Maybe I can beat Boinks in a game of checkers to get my mind off these books."

"Are you trying to drive me insane?" yells King Toot. "Why do you keep using the same word, *beat,* over and over, but every time you say it, it has a different meaning?"

"Lots of words have multiple meanings," says Tennessee.

Inter–Activity

King Toot is confused by words that have more than one meaning. In his dictionary, most words only have one meaning. Tennessee needs you to add more meanings to his definitions.

1) Find each of the words listed on page 55 in your dictionary.

2) Add up to five more definitions after the definition provided from Toot's dictionary. You don't have to use the first five definitions listed—try to use as many different parts of speech as you can and list the part of speech before each definition.

3) Use one of the meanings in a sample sentence.

fix

1) *vb* – to place or fasten securely. _____

2) _____

3) _____

4) _____

5) _____

Sentence: _____

_____

legend

1) *n* – an unverified popular story handed down from

earlier times. _____

2) _____

3) _____

4) _____

5) _____

Sentence: _____

_____

public

1) *adj* – of, concerning or affecting the community or the

people. _____

2) _____

3) _____

4) _____

5) _____

Sentence: _____

_____

save

1) *v* – to rescue from harm or danger. _____

2) _____

3) _____

4) _____

5) _____

Sentence: _____

_____

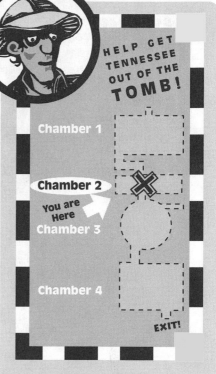

HELP GET TENNESSEE OUT OF THE **TOMB!**

Chamber 1

Chamber 2

You are Here

Chamber 3

Chamber 4

EXIT!

TOME TIP

Some dictionaries list the same word twice or three times in a row. They usually do this when a word has multiple parts of speech, and multiple definitions for each part of speech.

DICTIONARY

PREFIXES

"Gotcha!" yells Boinks, grabbing the bat that stole his funny bone. "I'll be taking this back, thank you very much."

Boinks puts his funny bone back in place, but it doesn't put him in a better mood.

"Ever since Tennessee found our tomb, I have been getting into a lot of trouble with King Toot," he says to himself. "First he got mad at me for no reason, and then he forgot to tell me about the flesh-eating bats. What's next? He forgets to tell me about the jester-eating lions?"

"I have to make sure Tennessee makes it out of here and fast!" he realizes. Boinks runs back to Chamber 2.

"It looks like I have finally stumped Tennessee!" King Toot brags. "He cannot figure out the meanings to a bunch of prefixes! The last explorer had trouble with this one too," he says, motioning to the pile of bones propped against the room's wall.

"Just give me a few minutes," says Tennessee. The batteries in his PalmSpring 7000 have worn out! Boinks sees his handheld computer and the two batteries he is fiddling with.

"Try these," Boinks whispers, handing Tennessee two fresh Durasmell AA batteries. "I'll explain later."

Inter–Activity

Tennessee needs your help getting past the prefixes that doomed the explorer who came before him.

1) Look up the meaning of each of the following prefixes in your dictionary.

2) Once you have found the meaning of each prefix, add it to the words below and write the new meanings. Try to figure out the meaning of the new word yourself, before you look it up in your dictionary.

Prefix
un–

Meaning _____

Examples	*New Word*	*New Meaning*
kind	**unkind**	**not nice**
attractive	_____	_____
interested	_____	_____

Prefix
pre–

Meaning _____

Examples	*New Word*	*New Meaning*
cook	_____	_____
determine	_____	_____
occupy	_____	_____

Prefix
post–

Meaning _____

Examples	*New Word*	*New Meaning*
date	_____	_____
meridian	_____	_____
script	_____	_____

Prefix
dis–

Meaning _____

Examples	*New Word*	*New Meaning*
belief	_____	_____
service	_____	_____
advantage	_____	_____

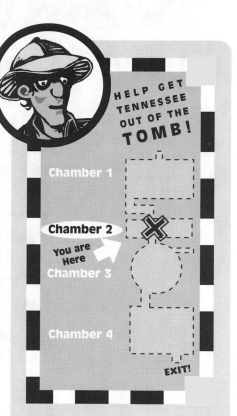

HELP GET
TENNESSEE
OUT OF THE
TOMB!

Chamber 1

Chamber 2

You are
Here
Chamber 3

Chamber 4

EXIT!

TOME TIP

Most dictionaries
do not give definitions for
words that use prefixes.
Instead, they list all of
the *un-* words or all of the
dis- words, for example,
and then direct you to the
root word for the definition.

DICTIONARY

SUFFIXES

Very impressive Tennessee!" King Toot says. "You have made it farther than the last guy who tumbled into our tomb. Now, if you will solve my dictionary's suffix problem, I will go check on dinner. I have sandcakes in the oven!"

"Where did you get fresh batteries?" Tennessee asks Boinks when the boy king is out of earshot.

"Promise you won't tell?"

"Yes, yes."

Boinks presses the nose on an Egyptian wall painting. The two are flipped into a secret room full of video games and electronics!

"One day a truck got sucked into the quicksand and fell into the tomb. The driver wasn't in it, he must have left the truck to look for help. Anyway, it was full of this stuff! Games, TVs, batteries! I set all of the electronics up in here and rolled the truck down into our Giant Hole to Nowhere."

"Why didn't you tell King Toot?" Tennessee asks.

"The Bean Turtle champion?" Boinks replies. "Do you realize how many times I have heard his Bean Turtle stories? If he beat me at *Sonic The Hedgehog,* I'd never hear the end of it. Shh! I hear him coming!"

Boinks presses the nose button and they are back in the tomb.

"The sandcakes need a little longer," King Toot smiles. "How are those suffixes coming along?"

Inter–Activity

Tennessee has replaced the batteries in his PalmSpring 7000. Help him by updating the suffixes and words in King Toot's dictionary.

1) Look up the meaning of each of the following suffixes in your dictionary.

2) Add each suffix to the words below and write the meanings of the new words. Try to figure out the new meaning yourself before you look it up in your dictionary.

> **Note:** A "y" at the end of a word usually changes to an "i" when you add a suffix.

Suffix -ness	Meaning		
		New Word	New Meaning
Examples			
moody		**moodiness**	**emotional attitude**
bright		_____	_____
happy		_____	_____

Suffix -able	Meaning		
		New Word	New Meaning
Examples			
laugh		_____	_____
remark		_____	_____
break		_____	_____

Suffix -ly	Meaning		
		New Word	New Meaning
Examples			
normal		_____	_____
hour		_____	_____
casual		_____	_____

HELP GET TENNESSEE OUT OF THE TOMB!

Chamber 1

Chamber 2

You are Here

Chamber 3

Chamber 4

EXIT!

TOME TEST

Here is one more suffix. Look it up in your dictionary, write down the definition, then give an example of a word that uses the suffix.

Suffix: -y

Definition: _____

Example: _____

_____

_____

_____

DICTIONARY

WORD ORIGINS 1

Boinks!" yells King Toot. "What is this?"

King Toot picks a *Sonic The Hedgehog* CD-ROM up off the floor.

"Um uh I um uh," Boinks stutters.

"It's mine!" Tennessee blurts out.

King Toot opens the case. "Ah, I see," he says holding the disc in the air. "It is a modern-day silver plate. I threw the silver plate, too! I was not only a champion at Bean Turtle, but also at the Silver Plate Toss."

Tennessee and Boinks each breathe a sigh of relief.

"The Greeks called it a *disc*," Tennessee explains. "And the discus throw is still a game at the modern Olympics. Remember the Olympics? I wrote down all of the gold medal winners when we updated your almanac."

"Of course I remember," King Toot replies.

"The English language kind of works like sports do," Tennessee explains. "Words, like sports, get handed down and changed from country to country, and from generation to generation."

"I see," says the boy king. "Then we should find out where all the words in my dictionary come from, and then we should toss some silver plates!"

Inter–Activity

Tennessee needs your help finding the origins of a bunch of words in King Toot's dictionary.

1) For each of the abbreviations on the next page, spell out the language that the abbreviation stands for.

2) Look up the list of words beside the languages and connect each word to its language of origin. Tennessee has done one to get you started.

Note: Some smaller dictionaries do not provide word origins. If you are using a pocket-sized edition, go to your school library or a bookstore and use a full-sized dictionary for this activity.

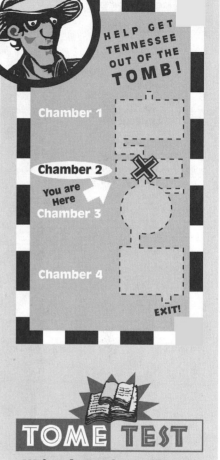

HELP GET TENNESSEE OUT OF THE **TOMB!**

Chamber 1

Chamber 2

You are Here
Chamber 3

Chamber 4

EXIT!

Abbreviation	Language of Origin	Words
Du or D		● ealdorman
F or Fr		
Gk		● gaff
Heb	Hebrew ●	
It or Ital		● hybrid
J or Jp		
L or Lat		● nori
ME		
ML		
Norw		● portrait
OE		
OFr or OF		● munch
OHG		
ON		● Doukhobor
OS		
Per or Pers		
Sp or Span		● Ishmael

TOME TEST

Write down three of your favorite foods. Look up the language of origin for each of the words and write down the abbreviation for the language.

Food	Language of Origin
1.	
2.	
3.	

DICTIONARY

RESOURCE
English language dictionary

SKILL
Finding out how old a word is

WORD ORIGINS 2

I haven't lost my touch!" brags the happy boy king after he, Tennessee, and Mel Boinks each toss a silver plate as far as they can. "I am the champion!"

"What's that smell?" Tennessee asks.

"Your sandcakes are burning!" yells Boinks. "I'll get them!"

"I hope they aren't too burned," says King Toot. "Oh well, if they are, we'll just dump them in the Giant Hole to No-"

King Toot stops himself short.

"The Giant Hole to No-?" Tennessee repeats.

"Drat," says Toot. "I did not want you to know about that. Okay, the Giant Hole to Nowhere! It is a big hole, it seems bottomless, but we don't know. We throw stuff down there and never see it again."

"It's like a big drainpipe, I guess," says Tennessee.

"A big what? What's a *drainpipe*?" asks King Toot.

"You know, a sewer, where water and stuff run to."

"I know what a sewer is!" the boy king barks. "But a drainpipe, did you make this word up?"

"No, it's just a newer word. Newer than sewer."

Inter-Activity

Tennessee needs you to find the first time the following words were used.

1) Look up each word and find its date of origin (the year or century it was first used).

2) Once you have found all of the dates, put the words in chronological order on the English language timeline along the bottom of the page.

year

PAST

word

Note: If a word has more than one definition entry, use the oldest usage.

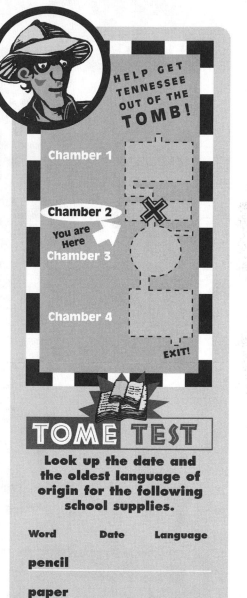

HELP GET TENNESSEE OUT OF THE TOMB!

Chamber 1

Chamber 2

You are Here

Chamber 3

Chamber 4

EXIT!

Word	Year/Century
car seat	
computer	
dictionary	
garbage	
jackhammer	
Internet	
jungle gym	
popcorn	
raffle	
scorpion	

TOME TEST

Look up the date and the oldest language of origin for the following school supplies.

Word	Date	Language
pencil		
paper		
chalk		

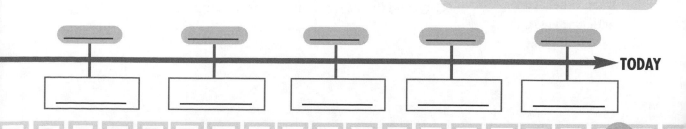

TODAY

DICTIONARY

RESOURCE

English language dictionary

SKILL

Tracing a word's origins

LATIN AND GREEK ROOTS

Mel Boinks returns to the room with a silver plate piled high with burnt sandcakes.

"I couldn't save them," he moans. "If you tell me the ingredients, I can make us some more."

"That is very generous of you Boinks," says King Toot. "Of course, you need sand, that is the *root* of any good sandcake. Then you add water, dirt, and gravel, and top it off with a spoonful of zerbits."

"The gunk from underneath your toenails!" yells a disgusted Tennessee.

"That is my secret ingredient, so don't go telling anyone."

"Believe me, I won't," says Tennessee. "But I also have to say, the way you just described making sandcakes is the way the English language is built. A word usually has a root language, and then a bunch of other languages are added like ingredients to that root word until you have the final, modern English word."

"Well, sandcakes always have sand in them," says Toot. "Do English words always come from one language?"

"No. Not always," explains Tennessee. "But lots of the words come from either Latin or Greek—or both!"

Inter-Activity

Tennessee needs you to find which language a bunch of words came from: Greek, Latin, both languages, or neither of them.

1) Look up the definitions of the words on page 65.

2) Read their word histories carefully, and trace them back to either Greek, Latin, both languages, or neither.

3) Circle the correct answer following the word.

Word | Source

Word	Source			
attention	Greek	Latin	Both	Neither
bland	Greek	Latin	Both	Neither
cane	Greek	Latin	Both	Neither
dull	Greek	Latin	Both	Neither
enigma	Greek	Latin	Both	Neither
foot	Greek	Latin	Both	Neither
genius	Greek	Latin	Both	Neither
harmony	Greek	Latin	Both	Neither
igloo	Greek	Latin	Both	Neither
jungle	Greek	Latin	Both	Neither
krypton	Greek	Latin	Both	Neither
language	Greek	Latin	Both	Neither
meteor	Greek	Latin	Both	Neither
night	Greek	Latin	Both	Neither
oil	Greek	Latin	Both	Neither
partridge	Greek	Latin	Both	Neither
quail	Greek	Latin	Both	Neither
rig	Greek	Latin	Both	Neither
scene	Greek	Latin	Both	Neither
tetrad	Greek	Latin	Both	Neither
usher	Greek	Latin	Both	Neither
venom	Greek	Latin	Both	Neither
warm	Greek	Latin	Both	Neither
X ray	Greek	Latin	Both	Neither
yogurt	Greek	Latin	Both	Neither
zodiac	Greek	Latin	Both	Neither

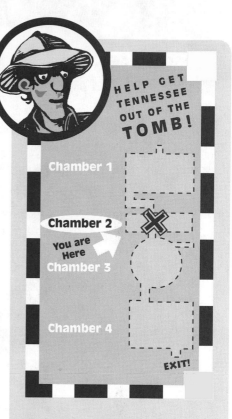

HELP GET TENNESSEE OUT OF THE TOMB!

Chamber 1

Chamber 2

You are Here

Chamber 3

Chamber 4

EXIT!

TOME TEST

Turn to a page in your dictionary. Pick any ten words in a row and count the number of words with Greek or Latin origins.

Which language, Greek or Latin, appears more times in your group of words?

DICTIONARY

KING TOOT'S HAZARDOUS PUZZLE OF PAIN 2

M y dictionary is much better," admits King Toot. "And I thank you. But there is one word in my old dictionary that must have a perfect definition, because it is a word that means a lot to this old Egyptian mummy."

"Are you talking about the word *zerbits*?" asks Boinks.

"Zerbits *are* important, but no," King Toot corrects. "I am talking about one of our civilization's great contributions to the world!"

"Sandcakes?" Boinks guesses.

"No!" yells King Toot.

"Bean Turtle?"

"Guess again!"

"The pyramids?" tries Tennessee,

"Yes!" the boy king exclaims. "Very good! The ancient Egyptians built the pyramids, you know."

"I do know," Tennessee says. "But how they built them is still one of the great mysteries of the world."

"I bet you would like to know how we built them so big and so tall using only our backs and our brains," teases the boy king.

"Yes! How?" begs Tennessee.

"Practice, practice, practice!" Boinks laughs. "Now give me a tasty sandcake. Mmm, that's good. Just the right amount of zerbits!"

Inter–Activity

Tennessee needs to write the perfect definition of the word *pyramid* to make it to the next tome chamber. Answer the following questions using your dictionary's definition of the word *pyramid*.

By completing King Toot's Hazardous Puzzle of Pain and answering the Extra Hazardous Password Question, Tennessee can make it to Chamber 3: The World Atlas.

1. Which syllable is stressed in the pronunciation of the word *pyramid*?

_____

2. How many different parts of speech are there for the word *pyramid*?

_____

3. What are those parts of speech?

_____

4. How many parts of speech can be formed by adding suffixes to the word *pyramid*? What are the parts of speech?

_____

_____

5. What suffix forms of the word *pyramid* does your dictionary list?

_____

_____

6. Are any prefix forms given in your dictionary's definition of *pyramid*?

_____

7. What language or languages does the word *pyramid* come from?

_____

_____

8. Is there a Latin root for the word *pyramid*? If so, what is it?

_____

_____

9. Which definition of *pyramid* does Toot's dictionary probably already have?

_____

_____

_____

10. Copy down one definition of *pyramid* that you didn't already know.

_____

_____

_____

EXTRA HAZARDOUS PASSWORD QUESTION

If you take *–yramid* off of the word *pyramid* and replace it with *–ercent*, what word do you get?

Password 2

_____

CHAMBER 3

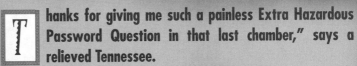

T hanks for giving me such a painless Extra Hazardous Password Question in that last chamber," says a relieved Tennessee.

"Do not mention it," replies Toot. "I felt badly beating you so soundly in our game of Silver Plate Toss. Plus, I really needed you to get to my atlas. As you noticed, that last guy did not make it past the dictionary chamber, so my atlas is a real mess."

Tennessee approaches a large table in the middle of the room. An old atlas and a stack of paper are on it.

Tennessee opens the atlas. All of the maps are of Egypt! There are no maps of any other countries at all! Tennessee's heart starts beating faster. How will he ever get this atlas in shape?

"I really need your help this time," he types into his PalmSpring 7000.

"What are you playing with there?" King Toot asks, noticing Tennessee's handheld computer for the first time.

"Oh, nothing," Tennessee stalls. "Just a . . . um . . . an electronic notebook! That's it! If I make it out of here, I want to write a book about you, so I'm taking notes!"

Dare to enter the third chamber of King Toot's Gauntlet of Giant Tomes!

Chamber 1

Chamber 2

Chamber 3

You are Here

Chamber 4

EXIT!

FOR STARTERS

Sit down with your atlas and go through it page by page. You will be amazed at all of the places in it.

How many of them do you recognize?

FINDING THE MAPS

Note: Your atlas has maps of large areas (Africa) that have a few details and maps of really small areas (Nile River Delta) that have lots of details. If you can't find what you're looking for on one map, look for a more detailed map of a smaller area.

"Great idea!" yells King Toot. "I really am a fascinating guy once you get to know me."

"Oh brother," sighs Boinks. "Do we have to listen to this now?"

"Silence, court jester!" commands the boy king. "Do not start getting uppity with me again. Or it is back to the flesh-eating bats with you!"

"Please, go on," says Tennessee. "And start from the beginning."

"Ahem," King Toot clears his throat. "I was born in Memphis to the King and Queen of Egypt, Froot and Tootsie Nile."

"You were born in Memphis?" exclaims Tennessee. "Me too! Memphis, Tennessee!"

"I was born in Memphis, Egypt!" the boy king says excitedly. "Wait. There are two cities named Memphis?"

"There are probably more than two," says Tennessee. "Lots of towns in the U.S.A. took their names from famous old cities. There's a Cairo in Illinois, a Paris in Texas, and a Delhi in New York."

"Very interesting," the boy king says thoughtfully. "My atlas should definitely include all of the world's cities named Memphis."

Inter-Activity

Tennessee needs you to look up a series of maps. Each map will provide more details about King Toot's hometown in Egypt and Tennessee's hometown in Tennessee.

1) Use the table of contents in your atlas to find the maps of the continents where Toot's and Tennessee's home towns can be found.

2) Use the map index to find the countries and states they live in.

3) Use the map index to find the city each was born in.

Finding King Toot's Tomb

Turn to the table of contents in your atlas. Find the page numbers for the maps of Africa. What are they?

Pages: _____

Turn to the index. Find the page number for the map of Egypt. What is it?

Page: _____

Turn to the index. Find the page number for the map containing the city of Memphis, Egypt. What is it?

Page: _____

Finding Tennessee's Hometown

Turn to the table of contents in your atlas. Find the page numbers for the maps of North America. What are they?

Pages: _____

Turn to the index. Find the page number for the map of the United States of America. What is it?

Page: _____

Turn to the index. Find the page number for the map of the state of Tennessee. What is it?

Page: _____

Turn to the index. Find the page number for the map containing the city of Memphis, Tennessee. What is it?

Page: _____

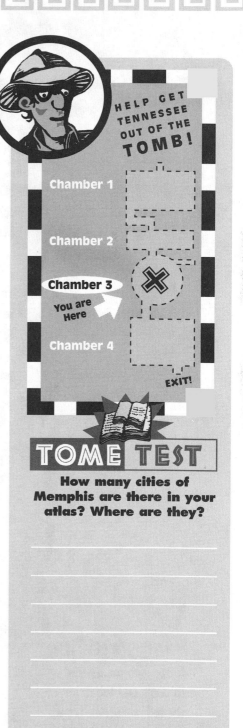

HELP GET TENNESSEE OUT OF THE TOMB!

Chamber 1

Chamber 2

Chamber 3

You are Here

Chamber 4

EXIT!

TOME TEST

How many cities of Memphis are there in your atlas? Where are they?

_____

_____

_____

_____

_____

_____

_____

_____

USING THE INDEX

"D oes the Memphis you are from have incredibly hot, dry days and a big river running past it?" King Toot asks.

"Not really," says Tennessee. "Once I get your atlas put together, you'll be able to tell exactly where Memphis, Tennessee is, what geographical features it has, and even a little about what the weather is like there."

"Oh goody," says the excited boy king.

"We'll start with your atlas's index," Tennessee continues. "The index in an atlas has to include more than just page numbers. The index also tells you the country or region the place is in, the page number, and the latitude and longitude."

To demonstrate, Tennessee labels the index entry for Memphis, Egypt.

Memphis, Egypt.....................*106* 29°52'N 31°12'E

Place   Country   Page #   Latitude   Longitude

Note: Some atlases also give map coordinates in their index entries, like this:

Memphis, Egypt..............*106* **J7** 29°52'N 31°12'E

Map coordinate

We'll cover those in the next activity, so don't use them in this activity.

Inter-Activity

Tennessee needs you to copy and label six index entries from your world atlas.

1) Find the index entries for the following places in your atlas.

2) Copy the index listing for each place.

3) Place each piece of information near the correct label, like Tennessee did for Memphis, Egypt. Use your map index's abbreviations key to figure out what kinds of places are identified by abbreviations like *r.* and *Oc.*

Agri River _____

(Place) (Where/What) (Page #) (Latitude) (Longitude)

Chandeleur Islands _____

(Place) (Where/What) (Page #) (Latitude) (Longitude)

Ivory Coast _____

(Place) (Where/What) (Page #) (Latitude) (Longitude)

Capitol Reef National Park _____

(Place) (Where/What) (Page #) (Latitude) (Longitude)

North Dakota _____

(Place) (Where/What) (Page #) (Latitude) (Longitude)

Midway Islands _____

(Place) (Where/What) (Page #) (Latitude) (Longitude)

HELP GET
TENNESSEE
OUT OF THE
TOMB!

Chamber 1

Chamber 2

Chamber 3

You are
Here

Chamber 4

EXIT!

TOME TEST

Find the list of abbreviations for geographical names and terms in your atlas.

What do the following abbreviations mean?

c. _____

vol. _____

b. _____

MAP COORDINATES

I hate to say this Tennessee, but all of those numbers and letters don't mean much to me," says King Toot.

"Me neither," agrees Boinks. "I'm going to go practice juggling."

"Stay away from my valuable vases!" King Toot orders.

"But I *promise* I won't drop them," says Boinks

"If I had a silver cat for every time you've promised not to break my vases, I'd be rich," the boy king replies.

"You *are* rich!" points out Boinks.

"Do not sass me!" King Toot warns, and Boinks sulks out of the room.

"Anyway, I was telling you about my Memphis, and I was hoping I would find out more about your Memphis," says the boy king. "But all you have given me are lines of numbers. This angers me, and believe me, you do not want to see me angry!"

"I think I have already," says Tennessee. "Just calm down. Maybe a map of Tennessee would help relax you."

"Yes, maybe it would," says King Toot. "I'll try anything. That Boinks is on my last nerve!"

Off in the distance, King Toot and Tennessee hear a CRAASSHHH!

"Sorry!" calls the juggling jester.

Inter–Activity

Tennessee needs you to write down the grid squares for a bunch of places on a map of his home state.

1) Study the map and list of places on the next page. Locate each place on the map.

2) Write down the grid square each place is in. The grid square for a place is the square where the letters on top (A, B, C...) and the numbers on the side (1, 2, 3...) meet. Tennessee has done the first one for you.

PLACE	GRID SQUARE
Nashville	E2
Knoxville	
Memphis	
Shelbyville	
Watts Bar Lake	
Evansville	
Pulaski	
La Follette	
Milan	

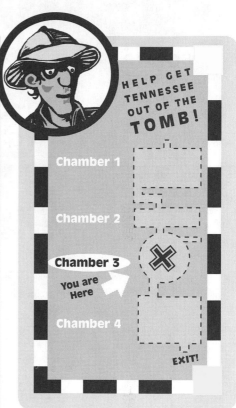

HELP GET TENNESSEE OUT OF THE **TOMB!**

Chamber 1

Chamber 2

Chamber 3

You are Here

Chamber 4

EXIT!

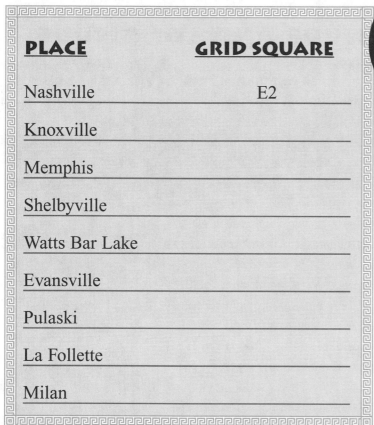

	A	B	C	D	E	F	G	H	I	J
1								• La Follette		
2		• Evansville			✪ Nashville				◉ Knoxville	
3			• Milan			• Shelbyville	Watts Bar Lake			
4		◉ Memphis		• Pulaski						

LATITUDE AND LONGITUDE 1

RESOURCE

World atlas with lines of latitude and longitude

SKILL

Using latitude and longitude coordinates

"So if I visit your country, maybe to buy some *new vases*, and I want to find Memphis, Tennessee, I ask someone to give me directions to B12?" asks King Toot.

"Not exactly. You can use *latitude* and *longitude* to find anyplace on Earth, including Memphis. That's how I found your tomb."

"Please explain," says the king.

"Okay. *Latitude lines* are drawn from east to west around Earth and are numbered by degrees north and south of the equator, which is at 0° latitude."

"*Longitude lines* are drawn north to south and are numbered by degrees east and west of the prime meridian. The prime meridian passes through the town of Greenwich, England, which is at 0° longitude."

"Each degree of latitude and longitude is then divided into 60 seconds, so any place on Earth can be labeled and located, like so."

latitude

longitude

	LATITUDE	LONGITUDE
Memphis, Tenn...	35°8'N	90°3'W
	degrees seconds	degrees seconds

"Great!" says Toot. "Now where can I go to find vases?"

Inter-Activity

Tennessee needs you to find the latitude or longitude of the following cities to within one degree. They all have vase shops.

1) Find maps of the Pacific Coast and Midwest of the United States in your atlas.

2) Locate the following large cities on the maps.

3) Approximate the longitude or latitude of each city to the nearest whole degree.

4) Look up the city in the index and find the EXACT longitude or latitude, including seconds.

Note: Each degree of longitude is divided into 60 seconds. So if a town is less than half way (less than 30 seconds) between 45 degrees of latitude and 46, you approximate it at 45°00′. If it is closer to 46 degrees, round up to 46°00′.

Estimate the latitudes of these cities on the Pacific Coast to the nearest degree, and then find their exact latitudes in your atlas's index.

	Approx. Latitude	Exact Latitude
Seattle, WA		
Portland, OR		
Sacramento, CA		
San Francisco, CA		
Los Angeles, CA		
San Diego, CA		

Estimate the longitudes of these cities across the Midwest, and then find their exact longitudes in your atlas's index.

	Approx. Longitude	Exact Longitude
Columbus, OH		
Cincinnati, OH		
Indianapolis, IN		
Chicago, IL		
St. Louis, MO		
Kansas City, MO		

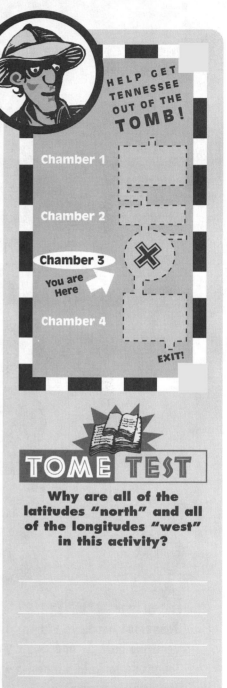

HELP GET TENNESSEE OUT OF THE TOMB!

Chamber 1

Chamber 2

Chamber 3
You are Here

Chamber 4

EXIT!

TOME TEST

Why are all of the latitudes "north" and all of the longitudes "west" in this activity?

LATITUDE AND LONGITUDE 2

I need to replace all the vases Boinks has been breaking," says King Toot. "I will start in the cities you located."

"Except you're trapped in your tomb for the rest of your afterlife because you're an Egyptian mummy," Boinks says, returning from his juggling practice.

"Drat! He is right. I forgot that for a second," says King Toot.

"Plus, I think if you did get out, there might be a few other places you might want to go first," adds Tennessee. "I've been all over the world, and I could recommend some really, really great cities and towns if you'd like me to."

"Yeah yeah!" Boinks chimes in. "Are there places where jugglers and clowns are treated like kings?"

"Um, not really," says Tennessee. "But in lots of big cities, you see jugglers and clowns on the streets, entertaining the people."

"You mean they don't entertain the king—just the ordinary people? What do ordinary people laugh at?"

"Who cares!" yells King Toot.

"Oh, you know, the usual stuff," says Tennessee. "Slipping on banana peels, knock-knock jokes, *The Osbournes*."

"You mean *Ozzy Osbourne*? The heavy metal madman?" Boinks asks.

"What are you talking about?" demands King Toot. "Do you know things about the outside world that I do not?"

Inter-Activity

Tennessee needs you to read the latitude and longitude for a bunch of big cities in your atlas's index of maps.

1) Turn to your atlas's index of maps.

2) Look up the latitude and longitude of the following cities.

3) Once you have filled in the coordinates for each city, answer the questions that follow.

TENNESSEE'S REALLY NEAT CITY RECOMMENDATIONS

HELP GET TENNESSEE OUT OF THE TOMB!

Chamber 1

Chamber 2

Chamber 3

You are Here

Chamber 4

EXIT!

	Latitude	Longitude
Beijing, China		
Delhi, India		
Johannesburg, South Africa		
London, England		
Moscow, Russia		
New York, New York		
Paris, France		
Tokyo, Japan		

Which city is furthest south? _____

Which city is furthest north? _____

Which city is furthest east? _____

Which city is furthest west? _____

TOME TEST

Choose three cities that mean something to you (places where you have lived, where your grandparents live, etc.) and find the latitude and longitude for each in your atlas's index of maps.

Place	_Lat./Long._
1.	
2.	
3.	

ATLAS

CITIES AND TOWNS

No no no," Boinks says quickly, "it was just a guess," not telling the king about the rock and roll CDs that were in the truck that fell into the tomb.

Tennessee sees the jester is in trouble.

"Knock knock!" Tennessee interrupts.

"Who's there?" King Toot and Boinks say together.

"Atlas."

"Atlas who?"

"At*las* we know where to find jugglers and vases!"

"Where?" both say together again.

"The big cities! And you can see on an atlas which towns have more people than others. An atlas shows different city sizes by using different kinds of dots and different-sized letters."

◉ 1,000,000 and over

◎ 250,000 to 1,000,000

⊙ 100,000 to 250,000

● 25,000 to 100,000

○ 0 to 25,000

Inter–Activity

Tennessee needs you to look at the sizes of the dots next to city and town names and figure out which places are large and which are small.

1) Find your atlas's legend page and bookmark it. (Your atlas has a legend that shows you the relative sizes of towns and cities. The smaller the dot marking the town, the smaller the town is.)

2) Turn to the maps that contain the following towns.

3) Rank the towns from largest to smallest, based on the type of letters and dots used.

Note: If you can't find the cities easily on the map, go to the index, look up their grid coordinates or latitude and longitude, and find them the old-fashioned way.

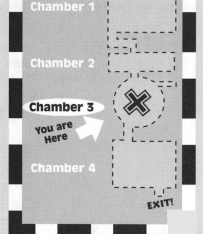

HELP GET TENNESSEE OUT OF THE **TOMB!**

Chamber 1

Chamber 2

Chamber 3
You are Here

Chamber 4

EXIT!

California (Western U.S.)

Cities	Size Ranking
Santa Cruz	
San Francisco	
San Jose	

Egypt (Nile Valley)

Cities	Size Ranking
Bani Suwayf	
Cairo/El Qahira	
Al Minya	

Cameroon (Central Africa)

Cities	Size Ranking
Douala	
Yaounde	
Kumba	

Australia

Cities	Size Ranking
Newcastle	
Wagga Wagga	
Sydney	

Alberta (Canada)

Cities	Size Ranking
Calgary	
Olds	
Red Deer	

TOME TEST

Turn to the map of your home state. List three cities that have the same dot size and type size.

State:

Cities:

1.

2.

3.

SCALE AND DISTANCE

By now, thanks to your help, Tennessee has added a lot of new information to King Toot's atlas.

"So, according to your maps, it looks like San Francisco and Santa Cruz, California, are about as close to each other as Paris, France, and Moscow, Russia," King Toot says. "In which two cities would you suggest I go vase shopping if I only have one day to do it?"

"Well, you should try the two cities in California," Tennessee suggests. "They're much closer to each other than the capitals of France and Russia are."

"But the distances on your maps are about the same! Have you made a mistake? Are you doomed to be with me for all eternity? Yippee!" exclaims the excited boy king.

"Not yet, King Toot," says Tennessee, and explains the concept of scale (much like we have done in the note below).

Inter–Activity

Tennessee needs to show King Toot the real distances between the following cities.

1) Get a ruler out.

2) Measure the distances between each pair of cities in either inches or centimeters.

3) Convert the scale distances into real distances.

Note: Scale is the ratio between the distance on a map and the actual distance in the real world. For example, one inch on a map can equal 2,500 miles in real life. To turn map distances into real-world distances, plug the distance on the map into the ratio and multiply the other side of the ratio by the same amount. *Example:* If Bragsville is 3 1/2 centimeters from Modesto on the map, and 1 centimeter = 100 miles, you would calculate the following distance:

3.5 x 100 miles = 350 miles from Bragsville to Modesto

How far would the following towns be from each other according to the following scales?

Scale: 1 inch = 100 miles
Palmdale to Felda

Felda

Palmdale

_____ inches = _____ miles

Columbus to Albany

Columbus

Albany

_____ inches = _____ miles

Scale: 1 cm = 10 kilometers
Bern to Eggiwil

Bern

Eggiwil

_____ cm = _____ km

Cork to Cobh

Cork

Cobh

_____ cm = _____ km

Scale: 1 cm = 250 miles
Riyadh to Pavlodar

Riyadh

_____ cm = _____ miles

Pavlodar

HELP GET TENNESSEE OUT OF THE TOMB!

Chamber 1

Chamber 2

Chamber 3

You are Here

Chamber 4

EXIT!

TOME TEST

Convert the following scales into real-world distances.

Scale: 1 inch=50 miles

Map Distance: 10 1/2 in

Real Distance:_____

Scale: 1 cm=1,200 miles

Map Distance: 3 cm

Real Distance:_____

PHYSICAL FEATURES 1

W hile Tennessee and King Toot are talking about vases, a bored Boinks starts practicing shadow puppets on the wall.

"This is a bird," he says to himself. "This is a cat, and this is a monkey."

Tennessee gets in on the fun.

"This is a mountain peak," he says. "This is a freshwater lake, this is a-"

"What are you doing?" Boinks interrupts. "You are the worst shadow puppeteer I have ever seen!"

"The only shadow figures I know are from the legend of a map," he explains. "Sometimes, when I am exploring, and I don't speak the language of the country I'm exploring, I use shadow puppets of the physical features you find on a map—airports, swamps, roads—to communicate with the locals."

"You are a strange one Tennessee," says King Toot.

"You'd never make it as a performer with those shadow puppets," Boinks says, then continues. "This is a goat, this is an apple, this is a boat."

"Maybe so," Tennessee admits. "But it was a shadow puppet I made of King Toot that led me to the map that led me to your tomb!"

Boinks and King Toot are playing and don't hear him.

"Do the cat again Boinks!" screams the delighted boy king. "Do the kitty!"

Inter-Activity

Tennessee needs to explain the physical features on a bunch of maps he has drawn in Toot's atlas.

1) Find the key to physical features in your atlas. It's usually identified in the table of contents as the *legend* or *map symbols*.

2) Now turn back to the maps.

3) Answer the following physical feature questions, using your atlas's legend.

Note: Remember to look for detailed regional maps if you can't find the information on larger area maps.

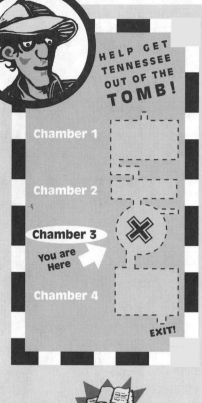

HELP GET TENNESSEE OUT OF THE **TOMB!**

Chamber 1

Chamber 2

Chamber 3

You are Here

Chamber 4

EXIT!

Map Legend
What do the following symbols represent on a map?

_____   _____   _____   _____

Map of Greenland
What is the dominant physical feature on your map of Greenland?

_____

Map of Hungary
What is the largest freshwater lake on your map of Hungary?

_____

Map of South Dakota or Northwest U.S.A.
What is the name of the big national park in South Dakota?

_____

Map of the Nile Valley in Egypt
What kind of physical features are the Pyramids and Thebes on your map of the Nile Valley?

_____

How many different kinds of lakes and reservoirs does your atlas list in its legend?

_____

What are they?

_____

_____

_____

_____

_____

ATLAS

PHYSICAL FEATURES 2

T hat was just wonderful, jester," says King Toot. "Your shadow-puppet skills are supreme."

"Why thank you, my great king," Boinks replies, bowing low.

"If you were to take your shadowy skills to the U.S.A., I am sure you would be the most popular puppeteer in the land," King Toot continues. *"Popular puppeteer*—say that five times fast!"

"Really? Do you think?" asks Boinks.

"Why, of course. You could start right in the middle of the country, right here," says the boy king, pointing to the state of Indiana. "Then you could ride your camel, Chester, across the country, delighting people everywhere you go."

"They might not let a camel on the highway," offers Tennessee.

"Why not!" says Boinks. "Do Americans hate camels?"

"No, it's just that cars go so much faster. Chester may not be safe on the road," Tennessee explains.

"You're just jealous because I am a great shadow puppeteer and you are a rotten shadow puppeteer!" says the angry jester.

"Show Boinks how he and Chester may get from place to place in and around Indiana!" orders King Toot. "Or you shall never leave this tomb!"

Inter-Activity

Tennessee needs to show King Toot the different ways he can get back and forth from various places in Indiana and the surrounding states.

1) Find the key to physical features in your atlas. It's usually identified in the table of contents as the *legend* or *map symbols*.

2) Answer the following questions about all the different ways to get from place to place. The latitude and longitude of each town are provided, so you can find them on your map.

1) What kind of road joins Indianapolis, Indiana [39°45' N, 86°08' W], and Louisville, Kentucky [38°15' N, 85°45' W]?

_____

2) Since King Toot has no driver's license, how can he get from St. Louis, Missouri [38°39' N, 90°15' W], to Cincinnati, Ohio [39°08' N, 84°30' W]?

_____

3) Can you drive on a single major road from Anderson, Indiana [40°05' N, 85°50' W], to Terre Haute, Indiana [39°25' N, 87°25' W]?

_____

4) What geographic feature do Chicago, Illinois [41°49' N, 97°37' W], and Milwaukee, Wisconsin [43°03' N, 87°55' W], have in common?

_____

5) What kind of road joins Decatur, Illinois [39°50' N, 88°59' W], and Indianapolis [39°45' N, 86°08' W]?

_____

6) Is Monroe Reservoir below Bloomington, Indiana [39°10' N, 86°35' W], freshwater or saltwater?

_____

7) What two rivers meet just south of Evansville, Indiana [38°00' N, 87°30' W]?

_____

8) Can you take a train from South Bend, Indiana [41°40' N, 86°20' W], to Indianapolis [39°45' N, 86°08' W]?

_____

9) Can you drive from Milwaukee [43°03' N, 87°55' W] to Grand Rapids, Michigan [43°00' N, 85°45' W]?

_____

10) Which town is bigger, Cincinnati [39°08' N, 84°30' W] or Louisville [38°15' N, 85°45' W]?_____

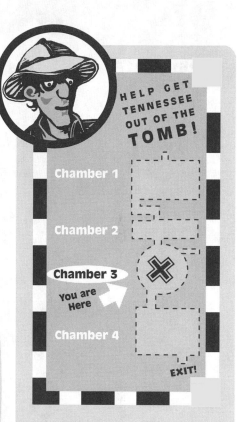

HELP GET TENNESSEE OUT OF THE **TOMB!**

Chamber 1

Chamber 2

Chamber 3

You are Here

Chamber 4

EXIT!

TOME TEST

Which states border Indiana?

_____

_____

_____

_____

ELEVATION AND DEPTH

W hat is this area that contains the state of Indiana called again?" King Toot asks.

"The Midwest," answers Tennessee.

"Does it have a lot of mountains on it?" King Toot asks.

"It has a few hills here and there, but no mountains, really," says Tennessee.

"Good," says Boinks. "Then Chester will have no problems."

"If your camel has trouble with hills, you might want to stay away from parts of the western United States," Tennessee cautions. "The Rocky Mountains and Sierra Nevadas would probably be hard on him."

"Chester is also a poor swimmer," adds Boinks.

"Then stay away from the coasts and the Great Lakes," Tennessee adds.

"What does that leave him?" King Toot asks.

"Well, the Midwest," says Tennessee. "The atlas is pretty good at showing how high mountains are and how deep oceans and lakes are."

"Then please add that information to my atlas," says King Toot. "For Chester's sake."

Inter–Activity

Tennessee needs you to interpret the colors your atlas uses to signify depths and elevations.

1) Find the physical maps of Australia and Tajikistan.

2) Use the elevations key off to the side of each map to answer the questions about elevations and depths at various places in each country.

Note: The color key for elevations and depths (also known as a relief map) is usually included in your atlas's key to features. It is also provided off to the side of most of the maps in your atlas.

Find the elevations and depths on the following maps.

Map: Australia

What is the approximate depth of the Bass Strait, off the coast of southern Australia, at 39°s, 146°E?

_____

What is the approximate elevation of Queensland at 25°s, 140°E?

_____

What is the approximate depth of the Indian Ocean at 40°s, 125°E?

_____

What is the highest elevation of Mt. Zeil at 23°s, 133°E in the McDonnell Ranges?

_____

Map: Tajikistan/Central Asia

What is the approximate elevation of Tajikistan's Pamir range at 38°N, 74°E?

_____

What color represents this map's highest elevations?

_____

What is the approximate elevation of the town of Dushanbe at 38°N, 69°E?

_____

What is the elevation of Mt. Pik Kommunizma at 39°N, 72°E?

_____

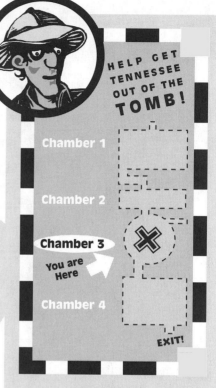

HELP GET TENNESSEE OUT OF THE **TOMB!**

Chamber 1

Chamber 2

Chamber 3

You are Here

Chamber 4

EXIT!

TOME TEST

How would you describe Tajikistan's terrain? Circle your answer.

A. Flat

B. Mountainous

C. Underwater

D. Underwear

ATLAS

WORLD MAPS: PHYSICAL

"I can tell from your maps that many parts of the world are very different from Egypt," says King Toot.

"Yep," Tennessee agrees.

"If Boinks is going to travel the world on his camel Chester, seeking fame as a shadow puppeteer, he is going to need to know everything he can about the world, so he doesn't go into any areas that are bad for camels to be in," King Toot explains.

"Yes, this is true," agrees Boinks. "I also need to avoid areas that are bad for mummies. We tend to get cold very quickly."

"Okay," says Tennessee. "So you probably want a map of the whole world's physical features, right?"

"If that wouldn't be too much trouble," says King Toot, "and if you ever expect to see the light of day again!"

"Look at this one King Toot!" Boinks says, holding his hands up to the light to make a shadow. "It's Chester!"

"Very good, Boinks!" laughs King Toot. "Now do the cat again. Please! Do the kitty!"

Inter–Activity

Tennessee needs to create a new physical world map for King Toot. Help Tennessee by studying your atlas's maps of the entire world.

1) Turn to your atlas's map of the physical world.

2) Answer the following questions using information from your atlas's physical world map.

Note: Most atlases have two world maps right in the beginning of the map section: one shows the world's physical features, another shows the world's nations and states (its political features).

Hint: The world map looks like a globe that has been flattened out.

1) What is the longest mountain range in South America?

_____

2) What is the most common physical feature of Antarctica?

_____

3) Using your map's key to elevations, what is the approximate depth of the Mariana Trench at 12°N, 144°E?

_____

4) Using your map, estimate the latitude and longitude of Amsterdam Island in the southern part of the Indian Ocean.

_____

Look up the actual latitude and longitude in your index. How close were you?_____

5) Which sea is part of the African continent's northern border?

_____

6) How high are the highest peaks of the Himalayan mountain range in the southern part of China and northern part of India?

_____

7) Name three places on your map that are on or near the Equator.

_____

8) What is the largest body of water within North America?

_____

9) Is Greenland located mostly north or south of North America?

_____

10) How many different oceans are labeled on your atlas? What are they?

Number: _____ Names: _____

_____

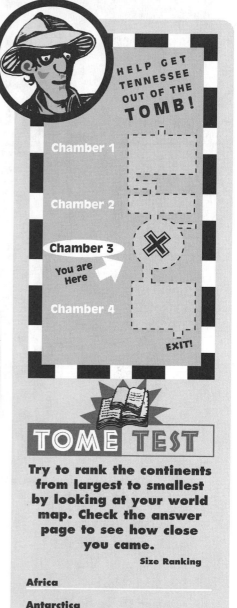

HELP GET TENNESSEE OUT OF THE **TOMB!**

Chamber 1

Chamber 2

Chamber 3
You are Here

Chamber 4

EXIT!

TOME TEST

Try to rank the continents from largest to smallest by looking at your world map. Check the answer page to see how close you came.

Size Ranking

Africa	_____
Antarctica	_____
Asia	_____
Australia	_____
Europe	_____
North America	_____
South America	_____

WORLD MAPS: POLITICAL

I 'm worried about all of this, King Toot," Boinks finally admits. "I mean, what if I go to a country that's flat and warm, but it has some sort of law against riding camels? What will I do then?"

"You tell them that if they have a problem, they should take it up with me, the great Toot!" shouts the angry boy king.

"No offense, oh great one, but you have been dead for a while now. That kind of threat might not work as well as it did 5,000 years ago."

"No? Well then, hmm. Tennessee? Any bright ideas?" King Toot asks.

"You could call ahead and see if the country has any anti-camel laws," Tennessee offers.

"You mean, write a letter and send a messenger on ahead with it?" Boinks asks.

"No, we have telephones now. They are machines that let you talk to another person over a long distance," Tennessee explains.

"Great! I guess all I need are those country names then, so I know who to call," says Boinks.

Inter-Activity

Tennessee needs to create a new political world map for King Toot. Help him by studying the world political map in your atlas—it shows the world's nations, states, and major cities.

1) Turn to the political world map in your atlas.

2) Answer the following questions using the information from your atlas's political world map.

Note: Your atlas's political world map may NOT have continent names. If you are unsure of which continents are where, check your atlas's physical world map for the continent names.

1) Which country on the South American continent has the largest land mass?

_____

2) Which country shares its name with its continent?

_____

3) Is Mexico part of North America or South America?

_____

4) Which ocean hosts the most island nations and states, the Atlantic Ocean or the Pacific Ocean?

_____

5) Which continent do Russia and China share?

_____

6) Which continent do Libya and Angola share?

_____

7) What is the northernmost country on your map?

_____

8) Which country separates 48 of the United States from Alaska?

_____

9) What is the capital of Indonesia?

_____

10) Which country is positioned directly to the south and east of Australia?

_____

HELP GET TENNESSEE OUT OF THE TOMB!

Chamber 1

Chamber 2

Chamber 3
You are Here

Chamber 4

EXIT!

TOME TEST

List all thirteen countries on the continent of South America.

1. _____
2. _____
3. _____
4. _____
5. _____
6. _____
7. _____
8. _____
9. _____
10. _____
11. _____
12. _____
13. _____

NORTH AMERICA AND THE U.S.A.

"I'm not sure the world is ready for my shadow puppet shows," Boinks says, scratching his chin. "They are pretty *wild* shadow puppet shows, you know? In one of them, I have a *cat* talking to a *monkey*."

"So what?" asks a confused Tennessee.

"He has a cat talking to a monkey!" King Toot explains. "Neither animal talks. And if they could talk, they most certainly would not talk to each other. That is what makes Boinks a genius!"

"He's right," says Boinks. "It's what makes me a genius. I think I should premier my shadow puppet shows in the U.S.A., and see if the people there are smart enough to understand my art. If the Americans get it, *then* I'll go on the road to Russia and Australia and Tajikistan."

Tennessee isn't sure what to say. It's like King Toot and Boinks have forgotten they are mummies. They aren't going anywhere! And there is no Chester—he died 5,000 years ago. Tennessee saw a hieroglyph about Chester's funeral on the wall in the first chamber!

"Okay fine," says Tennessee. "But I think we're getting a little off track here. I'm supposed to be helping you with your old atlas."

"Do you think us fools?" asks the angry boy king. "We're getting to that. We need a really good map of North America for Boinks and Chester, and then you can proceed to my Hazardous Puzzle of Pain!"

Inter–Activity

Tennessee needs you to answer questions about both political *and* physical features of North America.

1) Find the physical and political maps of North America in your atlas. (Most atlases have separate maps for the continent's physical and political landscapes, but some just combine the two onto one map.)

2) Answer the following questions using information from the North America maps in your atlas.

1) What are the four Great Lakes on the border between the United States and Canada?

_____

2) Which country borders Mexico—the United States or Canada?

_____

3) Which region of the United States has the highest elevations, according to the color key?

East   West

_____

4) What is the approximate latitude and longitude (within five degrees) of the easternmost point of the contiguous 48 states?

Approx.   Exact

_____

5) Which ocean borders the West Coast of the United States?

_____

6) Which country is across the Bering Strait from Alaska? What continent is that country on?

_____

7) What is the name of the river that empties into the Gulf of Mexico near New Orleans, Louisiana?

_____

8) What is the depth of the Gulf of Mexico along the coasts of Texas and Louisiana, according to the color key?

_____

9) Which two oceans touch both Canada and Greenland?

_____

10) Which city is further south—Denver, Colorado, or Pittsburgh, Pennsylvania?

_____

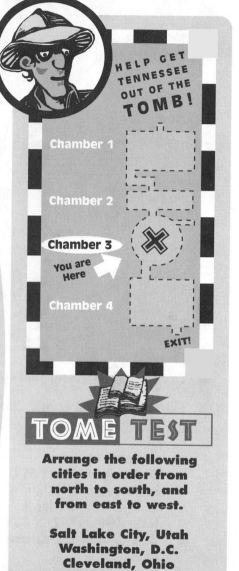

HELP GET TENNESSEE OUT OF THE **TOMB!**

Chamber 1

Chamber 2

Chamber 3

You are Here

Chamber 4

EXIT!

TOME TEST

Arrange the following cities in order from north to south, and from east to west.

**Salt Lake City, Utah
Washington, D.C.
Cleveland, Ohio**

North/South   East/West

_____

_____

_____

KING TOOT'S HAZARDOUS PUZZLE OF PAIN 3

RESOURCE
World atlas

SKILL
Using the whole atlas

Mel Boinks goes to practice his shadow puppetry, leaving King Toot and Tennessee to finish up the atlas.

"I need to tell you something," King Toot says. "I hate Boinks' shadow puppets, I know he's not going to be famous in the outside world, and I know Chester is dead. And he does too."

"Then why all that-"

"We need to do it to keep our sanity," King Toot interrupts. "We have been down here 5,000 years! Planning a shadow puppet tour gives Boinks something to look forward to, even if it is never going to happen. Now go and pass this last test, and you will only have one tome left. Then you get to leave and be rich and famous. And we will be left behind. Alone."

Inter-Activity

Complete King Toot's Hazardous Puzzle of Pain, which reveals the password needed to get to Chamber 4: The Thesaurus.

ACROSS

1 - the Brazilian city at 19°55's, 43°56'w
5 - the Swiss city at 47°8'n, 8°41'e (also a common breakfast food)
7 - Is the elevation at 29°n, 84°e low or high?
8 - the body of water separating Saudi Arabia and Egypt
10 - the river emptying into the Black Sea at 45°20'n, 29°40'e
13 - the north-south measurement on a map
14 - the northernmost continent on Earth
16 - the town in China at 51°n, 121°28'e
18 - the Japanese city at 34°24'n, 132°30'e
19 - the town in Libya at 26°49'n, 132°30'e
20 - an imaginary line that runs horizontally (east-west) around the center of the Earth
21 - the region in the former Yugoslavia that borders Macedonia

DOWN

1 - the islands off the southeast tip of Florida
2 - one of the most common modes of transportation drawn on maps
3 - the term for the largest body of water on Earth (there are four of them)
4 - the town in Saudi Arabia at 25°18'n, 45°52'e
6 - the city in England where east-to-west measurements start at 0°00'
9 - the southernmost country on the African continent
11 - the U.S. state at 40°n 116°w
12 - a measurement of height on a map
14 - a forest in Scotland at 56°51'n, 3°50'w
15 - the country that shares the northern border of the U.S.
16 - the U.S. state that borders both Lake Erie and Lake Ontario
17 - the Canadian province between the provinces of Manitoba and Quebec

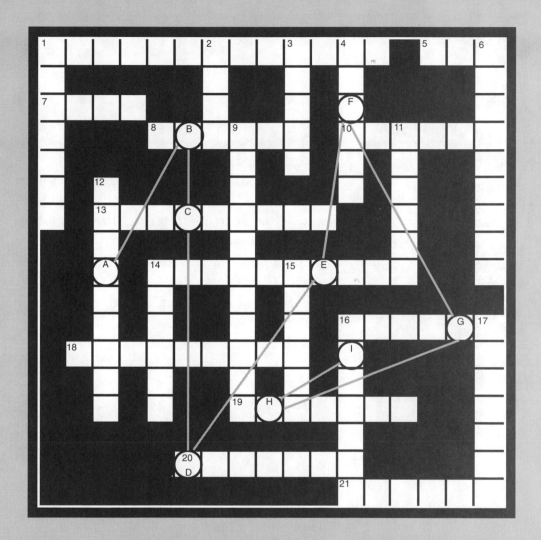

EXTRA HAZARDOUS PASSWORD QUESTION

What do the linked letters on your Extra Hazardous Puzzle of Pain spell?

Password 3

A B C D E F G H I

Tennessee can't believe it—just one more chamber to go! On the way to Chamber 4, King Toot leads the eager explorer through a museum of his life. Here he is, playing Bean Turtle. There he is, feeding his prized flesh-eating bats. Here he is making gourmet sandcakes.

They finally arrive at Chamber 4. Unlike the other chambers, this one looks lived in. It turns out it is Toot's study, where he has been working on his autobiography: *A Toot Uncommon.*

"Go ahead," says Toot. "Read it."

Tennessee reads a few paragraphs. It's not exactly bad, just repetitive.

"That is because I do not have a good thesaurus," explains Toot. "And since I am an ancient Egyptian, my English vocabulary is not very large."

"So, what do you want me to do?" Tennessee asks.

"Fix my thesaurus, and also fix my autobiography. If you make it out of the final chamber in my Gauntlet of Giant Tomes, take my book with you and show it to the world! It is all this lonely old mummy has left."

THESAURUS

Tremble before the fourth chamber of King Toot's Gauntlet of Giant Tomes!

Chamber 1

Chamber 2

Chamber 3

Chamber 4

You are Here

EXIT!

FOR STARTERS

Spend some quality time with your thesaurus, especially its *Synopsis of Categories*. Did you know there were this many categories of words in the English language?

THESAURUS

THESAURUS BASICS

"Toot, you have yourself a deal," says Tennessee. "Let's take a look at your thesaurus and see what I have to work with." Like his other reference books, King Toot's thesaurus is set up like a modern edition; it's just old and skinny. His thesaurus has two good tools for finding the synonyms inside it:

- the Synopsis of Categories (in the front of the book)
- the index (in the back of the book)

King Toot's index lists all of the words alphabetically. But instead of a page number beside the word, there is a *category.paragraph* number. For example, if Tennessee is looking for a synonym for *coffin*, he looks up *coffin* in the index and finds this:

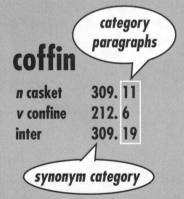

coffin

n casket	309.	11
v confine	212.	6
inter	309.	19

category paragraphs

synonym category

Synonyms for *casket* are in *eleventh* paragraph of category *309*. Synonyms for *confine* are in the *sixth* paragraph of category *212*. Synonyms for *inter* are in the *nineteenth* paragraph of category *309* (the same category that *casket* happens to be in).

"I start looking for synonyms using the category and paragraph numbers of the words that are closest to what I mean," Tennessee explains. "If that doesn't work, I look through the main category."

"Okay fine," says Toot. "Get to it."

Inter-Activity

Tennessee needs you to find (1) the category and subcategory numbers for the following synonyms in your index and (2) the name of the category each is found in. He did the first one for you.

Word	Synonym	Category.Paragraph #	Category Name
scare	fear	**127.1**	Fear, Fearfulness
moisture	rain		
car	railway car		
lounge	idle		
chase	hunt		
free	detach		
cat	feline		
skin	cheat		
surprise	attack		
weight	boxer		

HELP GET TENNESSEE OUT OF THE TOMB!

Chamber 1

Chamber 2

Chamber 3

Chamber 4

You are Here

EXIT!

TOME TIP

In a thesaurus, the range of word category numbers for each page appears where you would normally see the page number—in the upper right or left corner of the page.

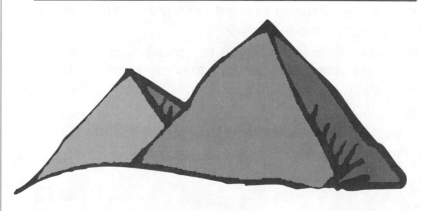

THESAURUS

RESOURCE

Thesaurus

SKILL

Becoming familiar with
word classes and
categories

WORD CATEGORIES

"Are you done looking through my thesaurus yet?" asks the impatient boy king.

"I guess, for now," Tennessee replies.

"Okay good. Then here is my book in a nutshell. *A Toot Uncommon* is the story of a boy who is born to be king and the country that loves him. We meet Prince Toot as a baby. He impresses his nanny with how loud and long he can scream. We watch him grow. As a three-year-old, he saves his pre-school teacher from a rabid ferret. As a nine-year-old, he composes a symphony for the Cairo Harp Orchestra. As a twelve-year-old, his flesh-eating bat Droolie wins First Prize at the livestock fair. Then tragedy strikes! His parents are poisoned by an evil servant, and the prince must take the throne at the age of thirteen!"

"This is great!" says Tennessee. "If you take this book to Hollywood, they'll surely make it into a movie!"

"I don't know what a movie is, but okay!" says the excited boy king. "Let's get to work right away because the story may be great, but my writing is terrible!"

Inter–Activity

King Toot's memoir has chapter titles that happen to match some of your thesaurus's fifteen *classes*. Tennessee needs you to write down three *categories* in each of the *classes* that would be helpful for rewriting Toot's chapters.

1) Turn to your thesaurus's word categories (sometimes called a *Synopsis of Categories*).

2) Find one of the word classes that matches or comes close to matching the chapter titles in King Toot's autobiography.

3) Write down three of the categories for each of your thesaurus's word classes. (Tennessee has filled out the first one for you.)

A TOOT UNCOMMON
BY KING TOOT

Chapter One
The Body and The Senses: A Childhood Full of Sweet Flowers and Silk Sheets
Three Categories:
1. **Unclothing**
2. **Fragrance**
3. **Cleanness**

Chapter Two
Feelings: My First Love: The Euphrates River
Three Categories:
1. _____
2. _____
3. _____

Chapter Three
Place and Change of Place: What I Did on My Summer Vacations
Three Categories:
1. _____
2. _____
3. _____

Chapter Four
Behavior and Will: Ruling My Empire With Class
Three Categories:
1. _____
2. _____
3. _____

Chapter Five
Human Society and Institutions: Egypt Embraces Peace and Harmony
Three Categories:
1. _____
2. _____
3. _____

Chapter Six
Values and Ideals: I Am Named Fairest King of the Year
Three Categories:
1. _____
2. _____
3. _____

Chapter Seven
Science and Technology: The Future Looks Bright To King Toot
Three Categories:
1. _____
2. _____
3. _____

HELP GET TENNESSEE OUT OF THE **TOMB!**

Chamber 1

Chamber 2

Chamber 3

Chamber 4

You are Here

EXIT!

TOME TEST

Name three word classes that your thesaurus uses that were NOT used in King Toot's chapter titles.

1. _____

2. _____

3. _____

THESAURUS

RESOURCE
Thesaurus

SKILL
Using the index

USING THE INDEX 1

"Can I see?" Boinks asks, looking over Tennessee's shoulder at King Toot's memoir. "Is there anything about me!"

"Of course there is," King Toot says. "But you cannot read it! Tennessee is just starting to . . . what *are* you starting to do, Tennessee?"

"There are a bunch of words in the first chapter that you keep repeating over and over and over again," Tennessee explains. "I have to find some synonyms for them."

"Repetitious words about me?" Boinks asks. "Like what? *Wonderful*? *Handsome*? *Talented*?"

"Uh, sure," Tennessee lies. "Those are in there. And so are other words, like *salad, mad,* and *bowling.*"

"*Salad*?" says Boinks. "But I don't like salad. Why would the world *salad* be repeated over and over again if I don't eat salad?"

"Because *I* like salad you selfish jester!" says King Toot. "This is *my* autobiography, not yours! You are in it here and there. I say very nice things about you and your camel, Chester, but the rest of the book is about me. *Me me me me me*! So stop being so selfish!"

"How could you possibly like salad?" Boinks asks.

"That's the straw that broke the camel's back!" yells King Toot, and chases Mel Boinks around the tomb with a big salad bowl.

Inter–Activity

Tennessee needs you to find two index entries for each of the following words and write down their category and paragraph numbers.

1) Look up the words on the next page in your index.

2) Write down the first two index entries that appear under each word in your index.

3) Write down the index entries, along with their category.paragraph numbers. (Tennessee has done the first one for you.)

INDEX ENTRY	CATEGORY.PARAGRAPH #

salad

1.   food   10.37

2.

green

1.

2.

jump

1.

2.

ascend

1.

2.

mad

1.

2.

bowl

1.

2.

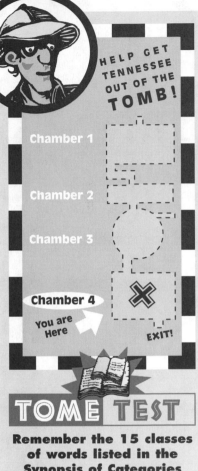

HELP GET TENNESSEE OUT OF THE **TOMB!**

Chamber 1

Chamber 2

Chamber 3

Chamber 4

You are Here

EXIT!

TOME TEST

Remember the 15 classes of words listed in the Synopsis of Categories in the front of your thesaurus? Write down the word class for each of the words you found synonyms for.

Word Class

salad

green

jump

ascend

mad

bowl

THESAURUS

USING THE INDEX 2

I 'm sorry, King Toot," an out-of-breath Boinks apologizes. "I don't know what got into me. I guess all that talk about my Shadow Puppet Tour of America got me all worked up. If I want to read a book about me, I should write it myself."

"Exactly!" says King Toot. "You do that. Now please leave me alone with Tennessee." Mel Boinks goes in search of a pencil and a pad of paper.

"I made a lot of progress with your book and your thesaurus while you were chasing your jester," Tennessee says. "I'm all the way to chapter four."

"That chapter is the turning point of the book!" says the boy king. "My parents are poisoned and I declare a new holiday in my honor. Tootmas!"

"Yes, well, that's fine, but your limited vocabulary really shows up in this chapter, too," Tennessee explains.

"Oh no, that is terrible," cries King Toot. "If the most important chapter is also the worst chapter, who will ever read my book?

"You're right," says Tennessee. "And what Hollywood executive will want to turn it into a movie? But we can make it better. I know we can."

Inter–Activity

You need to help Tennessee find synonyms for the words that King Toot uses over and over again in his chapter on ruling Egypt.

Use your thesaurus to find synonyms for the highlighted words in King Toot's chapter.

1) Turn to your index and find each of the **bold-faced** words.

2) Write one good synonym in the space provided beside the words. Important: For this activity, NEVER use the same synonym twice.

Chapter 4

BEHAVIOR AND WILL: RULING MY EMPIRE WITH CLASS

After I returned from my canoeing vacation down the Euphrates River, I had a country to run. My parents had been poisoned by an evil servant, so it was my turn to **rule** (_____) the **country** (_____). **Ruling** (_____) a **country** (_____) is very hard work. My father, King Froot, had a very hard time **ruling** (_____) the **country** (_____), so I knew it wouldn't be easy. The first thing I did was to name a new holiday after myself. I called the new **holiday** (_____) "Tootmas" and decreed that every year until the end of time, Tootmas would be a **holiday** (_____) celebrated on the day I was crowned king.

My loyal subjects were all very happy. In fact, I had never seen them so **happy** (_____). They were usually sad because they had to give me so much of their money, and if they didn't, I would have them thrown in jail or fed to the lions. But Tootmas was a **happy** (_____) **holiday** (_____). Men, women, and children lined the streets for the big parade past the pyramids. It was the biggest parade Egypt had ever seen. There were **big** (_____) statues carried on **big** (_____) platforms and **big** (_____) tables full of food and drinks. At the end of the parade, my royal jester Mel Boinks gave a comedy concert called *Boinks A Lot!* It was very funny. Mel Boinks can be **very** (_____) **funny** (_____) when he sets his mind to it.

I was **very** (_____) pleased with the concert — until Boinks told a joke about my tiny feet. Just because my **feet** (_____) are the size of a baby's doesn't mean he can **joke** (_____) about them. So I had him put in a cage and I gave people feathers so they could tickle him until he cried. Now that was **funny** (_____)!

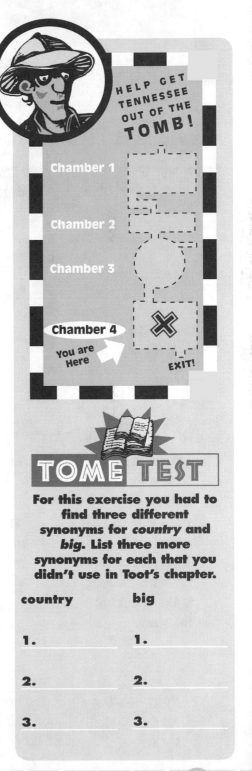

HELP GET TENNESSEE OUT OF THE TOMB!

Chamber 1

Chamber 2

Chamber 3

Chamber 4

You are Here

EXIT!

TOME TEST

For this exercise you had to find three different synonyms for *country* and *big*. List three more synonyms for each that you didn't use in Toot's chapter.

country	big
1.	1.
2.	2.
3.	3.

THESAURUS

RESOURCE
Thesaurus

SKILL
Finding synonyms

CHOOSING THE BEST SYNONYM

"We're done!" says Tennessee. "I edited your whole autobiography and added thousands of synonyms to your thesaurus!"

"Wait," yells Boinks. "What about a chapter about King Toot and me meeting you!"

"Oh no," says King Toot. "He's right. We need to add that. The seven chapters in my autobiography took me about 3,000 years to write, so writing another one should only take about 700 years."

Tennessee freezes. King Toot realizes Tennessee won't live that long. Then Boinks breaks the silence.

"I took the liberty of writing the last chapter while you guys were working on the rest of the book!" he says. Tennessee smiles, and King Toot looks relieved.

"Thanks Boinks," says Tennessee. "Let's have a look."

Inter–Activity

Tennessee needs to replace the second instance of each marked word with its BEST synonym. By BEST, Tennessee means the closest in meaning in the context of the story.

1) Write a synonym in the space provided beside each word. Pick a word you have heard of before. Words that aren't commonly used are usually NOT the best synonym.

2) Read the sentence aloud with the synonym you picked. If it sounds right, stick with it. If it sounds weird, try a new synonym.

3) Trust your instincts. If you think the word is a good synonym, it *probably* is.

4) If you have no clue, pick the shorter word. It is *probably* used more often in conversation and writing than a longer synonym.

Note: Picking a good synonym is more of an art than a science. With so many words that mean almost the same thing, consider the advice above for picking the BEST one from your thesaurus.

Chapter 8

MY NEW FRIEND FROM MEMPHIS

Life in my tomb wasn't going as well as I had planned. While I was lucky to have the funniest jester ever, Mel Boinks, by my side, I was still often sad. Plus all of the dried food my subjects had packed for me was getting really nasty. How would you like to eat the same **food** (_____) each and every meal? Can you even imagine what dried salad tastes like? Believe me, eating shriveled lettuce would make you **sad** (_____), too.

So imagine my joy when an explorer from the **future** (_____) fell into my tomb! Tennessee Toledo found my tomb while searching for my Field of Golden Fries. Of course I could not just let him have my treasure. I had to put him through several tests first. But he was up to the task. Tennessee turned out to possess a lot of knowledge that neither my handsome jester Boinks nor I **possessed** (_____). He was able to completely update the facts in my almanac, filling me in on all of the **facts** (_____) having to do with the modern world. Tennessee then helped me learn a new language, English, by working on my ancient dictionary. He also passed my atlas test, providing me with **new** (_____) maps of the outside world. And now, by using a thesaurus to **help** (_____) me finish my autobiography, *A Toot Uncommon*, Tennessee has earned the right to my Field of Golden Fries.

Only one more test remains. Part of me hopes he succeeds, because he is very nice. But another part of me hopes he does not succeed, so the intelligent Mel Boinks and I have another **friend** (_____) down here in the **tomb** (_____).

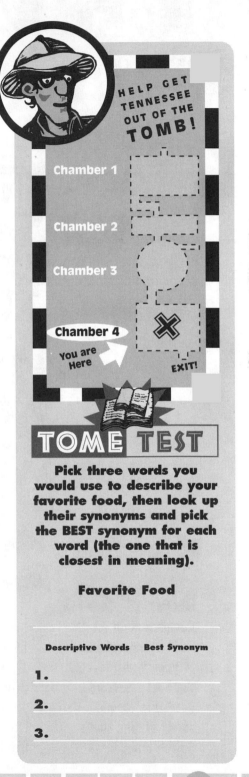

HELP GET TENNESSEE OUT OF THE TOMB!

Chamber 1

Chamber 2

Chamber 3

Chamber 4

You are Here

EXIT!

TOME TEST

Pick three words you would use to describe your favorite food, then look up their synonyms and pick the BEST synonym for each word (the one that is closest in meaning).

Favorite Food

Descriptive Words   Best Synonym

1. _____

2. _____

3. _____

THESAURUS

KING TOOT'S HAZARDOUS PUZZLE OF PAIN 4

Not bad Boinks, not bad at all," King Toot congratulates his jester. "I might have to change the part about me not liking dried lettuce, because I love dried lettuce, but everything else stays!"

"And I put in the synonyms for some of the repeated words," adds Tennessee. "So, are we done?"

King Toot and Boinks look at each other and nod.

"Yes, we are," says the satisfied boy king. "All you have to do is complete my final Hazardous Puzzle of Pain, and you are free to leave the tomb with as many of my solid gold french fries as you can carry."

"Do you want to make another bet on whether Tennessee makes it out or not?" Boinks asks.

"Sure! What do you have in mind?" King Toot asks.

"If he doesn't make it out, I will massage your feet every day for the next 1,000 years."

"And if he does answer correctly?"

"You and I switch places, and you are the jester and I am the king for the next 1,000 years!"

"You're on Boinks!" says Toot. "So get on with it explorer!"

Inter–Activity

Complete King Toot's Final Hazardous Puzzle of Pain, which reveals the final password needed to complete the secret of King Toot's Golden Fries.

For this Hazardous Puzzle, you need to fill in synonyms for some of the words in the lyrics to King Toot's Number 1 smash hit song: "I Was a Teenage Mummy." The synonyms you have to find all form the rhymes in the song, so when you pick your synonym it HAS to be the one that rhymes with the word above. Tennessee has completed the first lyric to give you an example. Good luck!

I WAS A TEENAGE MUMMY

(Sung to the tune of "California Girls,"
by Brian Wilson of the Beach Boys)

I was born to be a pharaoh in a hot and dusty place,
My name was Toot, I wore nice shoes, and had a pretty _____**face**_____.
Synonym for "front" or "visage"

I became a great Boy King. Yeah, I was born to be a star,
I had so many bodyguards I could sleep with my door _____.
Synonym for "open" or "gaping"

Yeah, being King Toot was cool, I got my pick of things to eat,
Some lizard tails, fishes' scales, and things too weird to _____.
Synonym for "retell" or "restate"

But being king was tough sometimes, good friends I could not keep,
Except the ones I paid to watch my horses and my _____.
Synonym for "ewe" and "ram"

I was the best king they'd ever seen, I was really overachieving,
But being king wasn't always fun, and then one day I stopped _____.
Synonym for "respirating" and "living"

Now I'm a teenage mummy, and beneath the earth I toil,
Some day I might come back to life, or turn into crude _____.
Synonym for "grease" or "lubricant"

I hope someone finds my Teenage Mummy World!
I hope someone finds my Teenage Mummy World!

EXTRA HAZARDOUS PASSWORD QUESTION

The password is the last word in the last verse:

Password 4

_____

TENNESSEE

"W oo hoo!" yells Boinks, taking Toot's crown. "I'm king!"

"Drat," says Toot, taking Boinks' jester cap. "I guess I'm the court jester."

Tennessee laughs. "Can I see the golden fries now guys?" he asks.

King Boinks claps three times and a wall slides into the floor, revealing the gleaming Field of Golden Fries and an exit from the Gauntlet of Giant Tomes. Tennessee fills his pockets and arms with the valuable treasure.

"It's been great fun, you two, but I've got to go. I'll let you know how it goes with your book, King Toot!"

"Goodbye Tennessee," Toot responds. "And thanks. Thanks for everything."

Tennessee turns from the pair of mummies, squints into the sunlight, pulls his wide-brimmed hat down over his forehead, and trudges through blowing sand that stings his skin like a million thumbtacks.

"Owwwwwww," he moans. "Owwwwwww."

But the pain doesn't bother him because Tennessee Toledo is already thinking about his next adventure . . . .

ESCAPES

Put the passwords from the four Tome Chambers together for the secret to King Toot's Field of Golden Fries!

_____ _____ _____ _____
Password 1 Password 2 Password 3 Password 4

The final door opens and there's the Field of Golden Fries and an exit from King Toot's tomb!

Read This First

You can do the Inter-Activities in this book with ANY reference book. BUT—and this is a very big BUT—if you use reference books that are different from the ones we used, your answers to the Inter-Activities will not match up exactly with the answers in the back of this book. THIS IS NOT THAT BIG A DEAL. The important thing is you get to know your reference books, no matter what brand they are. But if you want to be able to check your answers, by all means, use recent copies of the *World Almanac Book of Facts*; *Merriam Webster's Collegiate Dictionary: 10th Edition*; *Goode's World Atlas: 20th Edition*; and *Roget's International Thesaurus: 6th Edition*.

Read This Second

Some of the Tome Tests ask you for personal information, like your favorite foods, or who YOU would vote the next Miss America. For those questions, Tennessee has given his answers, but yours will probably be different (unless you also think Tennessee's girlfriend should be Miss America!).

Chamber 1
World Almanac

(Using *The World Almanac and Book of Facts 2002*)

Fact Finding 1
p.18

AEROSPACE
Memorable Moments in Human Spaceflight

AWARDS AND PRIZES
The Alfred B. Nobel Prize Winners

EDUCATION
Historical Overview of U.S. Public Elementary and Secondary Schools

EMPLOYMENT
Employment and Unemployment in the U.S.

WORLD EXPLORATION AND GEOGRAPHY
Early Explorers of the Western Hemisphere

HEALTH
Basic First Aid

HISTORICAL FIGURES
Ancient Greeks and Romans

METEOROLOGY
National Weather Service Watches and Warnings

NATIONS OF THE WORLD
Afghanistan

SPORTS
Sports Highlights

STATE AND LOCAL GOVERNMENT
Mayors of Selected U.S. Cities

CITIES IN THE U.S.
Akron, Ohio

UNITED STATES HISTORY
Chronology of Events

WEIGHTS AND MEASURES
The International System of Units

WORLD HISTORY
Chronology of World History

A sample of five subjects *not* on this list:

1. Travel and Tourism
2. Disasters
3. Offbeat News Stories
4. The Year in Pictures
5. Postal Information

Tome Test
Subject that interests Tennessee most:
World Exploration and Geography

Interesting Fact: Columbus never set foot on North America.

Fact Finding 2
p.20
These answers are for *T*, the first initial in Tennessee's name. We have listed all of the headings, but you only need to list six for your first initial.

ARTS, ENTERTAINMENT & MEDIA
Television
Theater
Tony Awards
TV

GOVERNMENT & LEGISLATION
Taft-Hartley Act
Tariff of Abominations
tariffs
taxes, federal
taxes, state
Teapot Dome
Temporary Assistance
  for Needy Families
Tennessee Valley
  Authority
Tonkin Resolution
Townshend Acts
Trail of Tears
Transportation,
  Department of
Treasury, Department
  of the
Treaties
Trust funds, Social
  Security
TVA
21-gun salute

PLACES
Tacoma, WA
Tahiti
Taiwan
Tajikistan
Tampa, FL
Tanganyika
Tanzania
Ta'u Island
Tennessee!
Territorial sea, US
Territories, US
Texas
Thailand
Thames River
Tibet
Tierra del Fuego
Timbuktu
Timor
Tobago
Togo
Tokelau Island
Toledo, OH
Tonga
Trinidad and Tobago
Tripoli
Tristan da Cunha
Tucson, AZ

Tularemia
Tulsa, OK
Tunisia
Turkey
Turkmenistan
Turks and Caico islands
Tutuila Island
Tuvalu

BUILDINGS AND LANDMARKS
Taj Mahal
Theme Parks
Three Mile Island
Ticonderoga, Fort
Trails, national scenic

RELIGION
Talmud
Taoism
Templeton Prize
Ten Commandments
Towers, freestanding

WEATHER
Temperature
Thunderstorm
  characteristics
Tidal Waves
Tides
Tornadoes
Tropical year
Typhoons

BUSINESS AND BUSINESSES
Tourism
Trade
Trans World Airlines
Travel and tourism
Triangle Shirtwaist Co.
  fire

SCIENCE & TECHNOLOGY
Tantalum
Technology
Telecommunications
Telegraph
Telephone
Telescopes
Titanium
Toxic chemicals
Trains

Transplants, surgical
Transportation
Trucks
Tunnels
24-hour time
Twilight

PEOPLE
Taft, William H.
Tarbell, Ida
Taylor, Zachary
Teachers
Thomas, Clarence
Thoreau, Henry David
Tilden, Samuel J.
Tito, Dennis
Tokyo Rose
Tripp, Linda
Trotsky, Leon
Truman, Harry S.
Tsars, Russian
Tudor, House of
Turner, Nat
Twain, Mark
Tweed, William "Boss"
Tyler, John

SPORTS
Taekwondo
Tennis
Thoroughbred racing
Tour de France
Track and field
Triathlon
Triple Crown
Triple jump

MISCELLANEOUS
Terrorism
Tet New Year
Thanksgiving Day
Theft
Third Reich
Thirty Years War
Time
Tires
Tobacco
Toothpaste
Top Ten News Stories
  of 1999
Tourrette syndrome
Trees
Turkey (meat)

21st century, start of
2-year colleges

Tome Test
Number of
research aids: 4

1. Table of Contents
   Page 3
2. General Index
   Page 8
3. Quick Reference
   Index
   Page 1008
4. Sports Quick
   Reference Index
   Page 1008

Reading Tables I
p.22
STATE INFORMATION FOR TENNESSEE
1. Section
Agriculture
Statistic
TN has 91,000 farms
covering 11,900,000 acres.

2. Section
U.S. Population
Statistic
In 1989, 15.7% of TN's
population lived in
poverty. In 1999, 12.7%
lived in poverty.

3. Section
Education
Statistic
In 2001, the median
SAT scores in TN were
562 for verbal and 553
for math, better than the
national averages of
506 for verbal and 514
for math.

4. Section
States of the Union
Statistic
The state population in

2000 was 5,689,283, up 16.7% from 1999.

5. Section
Environment
Statistic
Tennessee has 14 hazardous waste sites.

Dear King Toot,
Even though I've only been trapped in your tomb for a little while, I am incredibly homesick. You would be, too, if you were from a great state like Tennessee!
  Tennessee has grown a lot recently. 5,689,283 people lived there in 2000, up 16.7% from 1999. All those people in Tennessee are also getting richer. In 1989, 15.7% lived in poverty, but in 1999, this number fell to 12.7%. The students in Tennessee are also pretty smart, with median SAT scores of 562 for the verbal section and 553 for the math section. Both of these scores are higher than the national average. Tennessee also has a lot of farms – 91,000 covering 11,900,000 acres. Unfortunately, we also have 14 hazardous waste sites.

Sincerely,
Tennessee Toledo

Reading Tables 2
p.24
KING TOOT'S ALMANAC
Mummy Wrap Production
2810 B.C.E.   45,200,000 in.
2800 B.C.E.   46,300,000 in.
2790 B.C.E.   52,700,000 in.

Nile Delta Silt Count
2810 B.C.E.
96,000,000,000,000 grains
2800 B.C.E.
112,600,000,000,000 grains
2790 B.C.E.
67,400,000,000,000 grains

Papyrus Production
2810 B.C.E.
11,300,000,000 scrolls
2800 B.C.E. 9,400,000,000 scrolls
2790 B.C.E. 13,500,000,000 scrolls

Invading Hordes
2810 B.C.E. 56,300 soldiers
2800 B.C.E. 43,200 soldiers
2790 B.C.E. 145,000 soldiers

WORLD ALMANAC
National Debt/Surplus
for Year 2000
(millions of dollars)
+$236,993 =
+$236,993,000,000

U.S. Gross Domestic Product (GDP) for Year 2000
(billions of dollars)
$9,872.9 =
$9,872,900,000,000

U.S. Unemployment for Year 2000 (thousands of people)

5,655 = 5,655,000 people

Tome Test
Tennessee's Big Number
$9,872,900,000,000 (U.S. GNP)

Mel Boinks' Big Number
84,412,000,000
eggs produced in 2000

Current Events
p.26
BIRTHDAY #1
Date: February 22
Who: Jenny (sister)
CURRENT EVENT:
On February 22, President Bush said in his first press conference as president that he was concerned the Chinese were helping Iraq build weapons.

BIRTHDAY #2
Date: April 6
Who: Leonard (friend)
CURRENT EVENT:
On April 6, a jury in Los Angeles found an Algerian guilty of bringing explosives into the country that were meant to be blown up during the millennium celebrations.

BIRTHDAY #3
Date: May 25
Who: Sandy (mom)
CURRENT EVENT:
On May 25, Secretary of State Colin Powell urged the president of Zimbabwe to hold free elections.

BIRTHDAY #4
Date: June 24
Who: Louise (friend)
CURRENT EVENT:
On June 29, the former president of Yugoslavia, Slobodan Milosevic, was delivered to the Hague in the Netherlands where he was to be tried for a long list of war crimes.

BIRTHDAY #5
Date: August 8
Who: Georgia (girlfriend)
CURRENT EVENT:
On August 10, a land mine killed 250 people on a train in Luanda, the capital of Angola. The rebels who planted the mine then attacked the train, claiming it carried military equipment.

Tome Test
In a speech to Democrats, former vice president, Al Gore, declared "George Bush is my commander in chief" and said he supported his former rival.

Do you remember this happening? Yes ☒ No ❏

U.S. Government
p.28
YEAR:
2002
CURRENT PRESIDENT:
George W. Bush
His Staff
VICE PRESIDENT:
Richard Cheney
SECRETARY OF STATE:
Colin Powell
SECRETARY OF DEFENSE:
Donald H. Rumsfeld
SECRETARY OF TREASURY:
Paul O'Neill
ATTORNEY GENERAL:
John Ashcroft

YEAR:
1960
PRESIDENT:
John F. Kennedy
His Staff
VICE PRESIDENT
Lyndon B. Johnson
SECRETARY OF STATE:
Dean Rusk
SECRETARY OF DEFENSE
Robert S. McNamara
SECRETARY OF TREASURY
C. Douglas Dillon
ATTORNEY GENERAL
Robert F. Kennedy

YEAR:
1984 (Tennessee Toledo's birth year)
PRESIDENT:
Ronald Reagan
His Staff
VICE PRESIDENT
George Bush
SECRETARY OF STATE
George P. Schultz
SECRETARY OF DEFENSE
Caspar W. Weinberger
SECRETARY OF TREASURY
Donald T. Regan
ATTORNEY GENERAL
William French Smith

Tome Test
Three More Cabinet Positions:
Secretary of the Interior
Secretary of Agriculture
Secretary of the Navy

Elections
p.30
STATE: Tennessee

Senators	Party
1. Fred Thompson	(R)
2. Bill Frist	(R)

House of Representatives

Bill Jenkins	(R)
John J. Duncan	(R)
Zach Wamp	(R)
Van Hilleary	(R)
Bob Clement	(D)
Bart Gordon	(D)
Ed Bryant	(R)
John S. Tanner	(D)
Harold E. Ford, Jr.	(D)

YOUR STATE'S PRESIDENTIAL VOTING RECORD
STATE: Tennessee
YEAR: 2000
CANDIDATES (TOP 4):
1. Bush: 1,061,949
2. Gore: 981,720
3. Nader: 19,781
4. Browne: 4,284

WHAT PARTY DID THE WINNER REPRESENT? Republican
DID HE END UP WINNING THE GENERAL ELECTION?
Yes ☒ No ❏
WHO CAME IN THIRD? Browne
WHAT PARTY? Libertarian
WHO CAME IN LAST? Venson
WHAT PARTY? Independent
WHO WOULD YOU HAVE VOTED FOR? Nader

Tome Test
Who LOST each of the following presidential elections?

ELECTION YEAR	CANDIDATES	
2000	Bush	☐Gore
1992	☐Bush	Clinton
1980	Reagan	☐Carter
1960	☐Nixon	Kennedy
1948	☐Dewey	Truman
1912	Wilson	☐Roosevelt
1880	Garfield	☐Hancock
1844	☐Clay	Polk
1828	☐Adams	Jackson
1796	Adams	☐Jefferson

THE ENVIRONMENT
p.32
1. Three-Mile Island, PA – Big nuclear accident (1979)

2. Riverside-San Bernadino, CA – 93 days failed to meet air quality standards (1999)

3. New Jersey – 116 hazardous waste sites (2001)

4. Prudhoe Bay, AK – Has the nation's biggest oil field

5. Texas – 258 million lbs. of toxic releases (1999)

Tome Test
ENDANGERED SPECIES
Mammals 63
Birds 78
Reptiles 14

Populations
p.34

POPULATIONS LIST

	CT	IN	NV
1790	238	--	--
1800	251	6	--
1850	370,792	988,416	--
1860	460,147	1,350,428	6,857
1900	908,420	2,516,462	42,335
1910	1,114,756	2,700,816	81,879
1950	2,007,280	3,934,224	160,083
1960	2,535,234	4,662,498	289,278
2000	3,405,565	6,080,485	1,998,257

Tome Test
CAPITALS
Indiana—Indianapolis
Nevada—Carson City
Connecticut—Hartford

(There is a list in the index under "States – capitals.")

U.S. Facts
p.36
UNITED STATES 2000
Gross Domestic Product
$9,872.9 billion
Section: Economics

Gold Reserves
261.61 millions troy ounces
Section: Economics

Number of Farms
2,194 thousand
Section: Agriculture

Foreign Trade
Imports $1,218,022 million
Exports $781,918 million
Section: Trade and Transportation

Average Teacher Salary*
$42,898
Section: Education

Most Popular Newspaper
The Wall Street Journal
Circulation 1,762,751
Section: Arts and Media

Top Rated TV Show
Survivor
Section: Arts and Media

Most Popular Boy Name**
Michael
Section: Language

Most Popular Girl Name**
Ashley
Section: Language

Average Life Expectancy*
76.7
Section: Vital Statistics

*1999   **1990-1999*

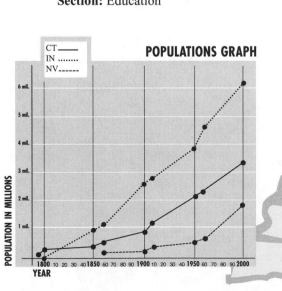

POPULATIONS GRAPH

CT ——
IN ....
NV ------

POPULATION IN MILLIONS

6 mil.
5 mil.
4 mil.
3 mil.
2 mil.
1 mil.

1800 10 20 30 40 1850 60 70 80 90 1900 10 20 30 40 1950 60 70 80 90 2000
YEAR

COUNTRY	MALE	FEMALE
Angola	37.36	39.87
Denmark	74.12	79.47
Morocco	67.2	71.76

World Leaders
p.38
Tennessee's world leaders.

GOVERNMENT LEADER:
JOSE EDUARDO DOS SANTOS
COUNTRY: Angola

GOVERNMENT LEADER:
SHAHABUDDIN AHMED
COUNTRY: Bangladesh

GOVERNMENT LEADER:
ALEJANDRO TOLEDO
COUNTRY: Peru

GOVERNMENT LEADER:
TANJDA MAMADOU
COUNTRY: Niger

GOVERNMENT LEADER:
HAYDAR ALIYEV
COUNTRY:
Azerbaijan

GOVERNMENT LEADER:
CHEN SHUI-BAN
COUNTRY:
Taiwan

GOVERNMENT LEADER:
THAN SHWE
COUNTRY:
Myanmar

GOVERNMENT LEADER:
TEBUROROTITO
COUNTRY:
Kiribati

GOVERNMENT LEADER:
FREDERICK CHILUBA
COUNTRY: Zambia

Sports Facts
p.40
Winter Olympics

EVENT: *Downhill: Men's*
ATHLETE/COUNTRY:
Bill Johnson/U.S.A.

EVENT: *Figure Skating: Pairs*
ATHLETE/COUNTRY:
Helene Engelman &
Alfred Berger/Austria

EVENT: *Figure Skating: Women's*
ATHLETE/COUNTRY:
Tara Lipinski/U.S.A.

EVENT: *Speed Skating:
Women's 500 Meters*
ATHLETE/COUNTRY:
Ludmila Titova/USSR

EVENT: *Speed Skating:
Men's 1,500 Meters*
ATHLETE/COUNTRY:
Andre Hoffmann/East Germany

EVENT: *Snowboarding:
Men's Halfpipe*
ATHLETE/COUNTRY:
Gian Simmen/Switzerland

Summer Olympics
EVENT: *100-Meter Run: Women's*
ATHLETE/COUNTRY:
Marion Jones/U.S.A.

EVENT: *50-Kilometer Walk: Men's*
ATHLETE/COUNTRY:
Raul Gonzalez/Mexico

EVENT: *Discus Throw: Women's*
ATHLETE/COUNTRY:
Maritza Marten Garcia/Cuba

EVENT:
100-Meter Backstroke: Men's
ATHLETE/COUNTRY:
Daichi Suzuki/Japan

EVENT:
100-Meter Butterfly: Women's
ATHLETE/COUNTRY:
Lynn McClements/Australia

EVENT:
Platform Diving: Women's
ATHLETE/COUNTRY:
Fu Mingxia/China

EVENT:
Middleweight Boxing: Men's
ATHLETE/COUNTRY:
Michael Spinks/U.S.

ANSWER PAGES

Awards and Prizes
p.42
Year: 1984
(Tennessee Toledo's birth year)

AWARD:
Nobel Prize in Medicine
WINNERS:
Cesar Milstien, Georges J.F.
Koehler, Niels K. Jerne

AWARD:
Nobel Peace Prize
WINNER:
Bishop Desmond Tutu

AWARD:
Pulitzer Prize in Fiction
WINNER:
William Kennedy, *Ironweed*

AWARD:
Pulitzer Prize in Poetry
WINNER:
Mary Oliver, *American Primitive*

AWARD:
Newberry Medal
WINNER:
Dear Mr. Henshaw,
Beverly Cleary

AWARD:
Miss America
WINNERS:
Vanessa Williams (resigned
7/23/84), Suzette Charles

AWARD:
Academy Award: Best Picture
WINNER: *Amadeus*

AWARD: Academy Award:
Best Actress
WINNER: Sally Field, *Places in
the Heart*

AWARD: Grammy Award: Album
of the Year
WINNER: Lionel Richie, *Can't
Slow Down*

AWARD: Grammy Award: Song
of the Year
WINNER: Tina Turner, "What's
Love Got to Do With It?"

**WHO WOULD YOU GIVE THE
FOLLOWING PRIZES TO TODAY:**
(Tennessee's choices)
AWARD: Nobel Peace Prize
WINNER: Undersea explorer
Bob Ballard

AWARD:
Academy Award: Best Picture
WINNER: *Shrek*

AWARD: Newberry Medal
WINNER: *Secrets of the Giant
Tomes Revealed*

AWARD: Grammy Award: Song
of the Year
WINNER: Lucinda Williams,
"Lonely Girls"

AWARD: Miss America
WINNER: My girlfriend Georgia
Smiles

Tome Test
Grammy Award:
Record of the Year 4
Academy Award: Best Actor 6
Caldecott Medal Books 8

*Extra Hazardous
Password 1*

Ten

King Toot's Hazardous Puzzle of Pain 1
p.44

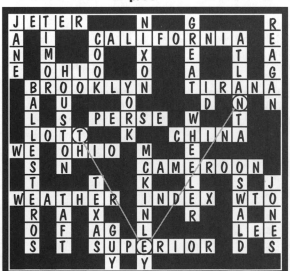

Chamber 2 Dictionary

(Using *Merriam Webster's Collegiate Dictionary: 10th Edition*)

Abbreviations
p.48
1. Third definition: With the wind.
2. Adverb.
3. First o: As in *oat* and *bone*.
Second o: As in *lemon* and *button*.
4. Grinkus
5. Handsome fellow.
6. Chemist and mathematician.
7. French.

SYLLABLES AND PRONUNCIATION
p.50
WORD
cello
YOUR PRONUNCIATION
CHELL-o
DICTIONARY PRONUNCIATION
'che-(,)lō

oblige
o-BLIJE
ə-blīj'

groggy
GROGG-ee
'grä-gē

papaya
puh-PIE-ya
pə-'pī-ə

igneous
IG-nee-us
ĭg'nē-əs

rambunctious
ram-BUNK-shuss
ram-'bənk-shəs

ancient
AIN-chent
'ān(t)-shənt

leader
LEE-der
lē'dər

uranium
yoo-RAY-nee-um
yu̇-'rā-nē-əm

scheme
SKEME
'skēm

migraine
MY-grain
'mī-,grān

telemetry
tuh-LEM-ih-tree
tə-'le-mə-trē

nuclear
NU-klee-ur
'n͞u-klēə r

vocabulary
vo-KAB-yuh-LAIR-ee
vō-'ka-byə-,ler-ē

beret
buh-RAY
bə-'rā

Parts of Speech
p.52

WORD	PARTS OF SPEECH
love	2 - noun, verb
from	1 - preposition
tire	2 - noun, verb
back	4 – noun, verb, adjective, adverb
school	2 - noun, verb
fair	3 – adjective, adverb, noun
caliber	1 - noun
point	2 - noun, verb
miss	2 - noun, verb
and	1 - conjunction
pass	2 - noun, verb
hey	1 - interjection
taste	2 - noun, verb
skin	2 - noun, verb

Multiple Meanings
p.54
FIX
1. *vb* – to place or fasten securely.
2. *vb* – to direct steadily.
3. *vb* – to assign.
4. *n* – a difficult or embarrassing situation.
5. *n* – the position of a ship or aircraft, as determined by obser-

vation or radio.

SENTENCE: I have gotten myself out of tougher *fixes* than being trapped in a tomb with a lonely mummy. Well, maybe not.

LEGEND

1. *n* – an unverified popular story handed down from earlier times.
2. *n* – a body or collection of such stories.
3. *n* – a person who achieves legendary fame.
4. *n* – an inscription or title on an object, such as a coin.
5. *n* – an explanatory caption accompanying a map, chart, or illustration.
SENTENCE: Elvis Presley is a rock and roll *legend*. He is the most famous rocker of them all.

PUBLIC

1. *adj* – of, concerning or affecting the community or the people.
2. *adj* – maintained for or used by the people or community.
3. *n* – the community or public as a whole.
4. *n* – a group of people sharing a common interest.
5. *n* – admirers or followers.
SENTENCE: When the *public* found out about the mayor's crimes, they voted him out of office.

SAVE

1. *vb* – to rescue from harm or danger.
2. *vb* – to keep in a safe condition.
3. *vb* – to prevent the waste or loss of; to conserve.
4. *vb* – *Theol* to deliver from sin; to redeem.
5. *n* – *Sports* an act that prevents someone from scoring.
SENTENCE: Mike Richter made a great *save* in the closing minutes of the hockey game, and the Rangers went on to beat the

Devils 4-3.

PREFIXES
p.56
Prefix
un – 1. Not. 2. Opposite of.

Examples
kind
unkind – not kind; mean.

attractive
unattractive – not attractive; ugly.

interested
uninterested – not interested; bored.

Prefix
pre – 1. Earlier; before; prior to. 2. Anterior; in front of.

Examples
cook
precook – cook before the final cooking.

determine
predetermine – to figure out in advance.

occupy
preoccupy – to get attention beforehand.

Prefix
post – 1. After; later. 2. Behind.

Examples
date
postdate – to put a date on something that is later than the current date.

meridian
postmeridian – taking place in the afternoon (PM).

script
postscript – a note attached to the end of a book or article.

Prefix
dis – 1. Not. 2. Absence of. Undo; do the opposite of. 4. Deprive of. 5. Use as an intensive.

Examples
belief
disbelief – absence of belief; refusal to believe.

service
disservice – a harmful action (the opposite of service).

advantage
disadvantage – an unfavorable position or condition.

Suffixes
p.58
Suffix
-ness – State; quality; condition; degree.

Examples
moody
moodiness – condition of being moody; emotional attitude.

bright
brightness – degree of being bright.
happy
happiness – state of being happy.

Suffix
-able – 1. Susceptible, capable, or worthy of a specified action. 2. Inclined or given to a specified state or action.

Examples
laugh
laughable – worthy of laughter.

remark
remarkable – worthy of remarking upon.

break
breakable – easily broken.

Suffix

-ly – 1. In a specified manner; in the manner of. 2. Recurring at a specific interval.

Examples
normal
normally – in the manner of being normal.

hour
hourly – occurring every hour.

casual
casually – acting in a casual way.

Tome Test
Suffix: -y 1. Characterized by; consisting of. 2. Like. 3. To some degree. 4. Tending toward.
Example: peppery

Word Origins 1
p.60

Abbr.	Language	Words
Du / D	Dutch	
Fr	French	
Gk.	Greek	ealderman
Heb	Hebrew	gaff
It / Ital	Italian	hybrid
J / Jp	Japanese	nori
Lat	Latin	portrait
ME	Middle English	Ishmael
MF	Middle French	munch
Norw.	Norway	Doukhobor
OE	Old English	
OFr / OF	Old French	
OHG	Old High German	
ON	Old Norse	
OS	Old Style or Old Saxon	
Russ	Russian	
Sp / Span	Spanish	

Tome Test

Food	Language of Origin/Abbreviation
pizza	Italian (It)
taco	Mexican Spanish (MexSpan)
hamburger	German (G)

Word Origins 2
p.62
TIMELINE →
Turn book sideways to see Tennessee's timeline answers

Tome Test

Word	Date	Language
pencil	14th c.	Latin
paper	14th c.	Greek
chalk	12th c.	Latin/Greek

Latin and Greek Roots
p.64

Word	Source			
attention	Greek	**Latin**	Both	Neither
bland	Greek	**Latin**	Both	Neither
cane	Greek	Latin	**Both**	Neither
dull	Greek	Latin	Both	**Neither**
enigma	Greek	Latin	**Both**	Neither
foot	Greek	Latin	**Both**	Neither
genius	Greek	**Latin**	Both	Neither
harmony	Greek	Latin	**Both**	Neither
igloo	Greek	Latin	Both	**Neither**
jungle	Greek	Latin	Both	**Neither**
krypton	**Greek**	Latin	Both	Neither
language	Greek	**Latin**	Both	Neither
meteor	Greek	Latin	**Both**	Neither
night	Greek	**Latin**	Both	Neither

oil	Greek	Latin	**Both**	Neither
partridge	Greek	Latin	**Both**	Neither
quail	Greek	**Latin**	Both	Neither
rig	Greek	Latin	Both	**Neither**
scene	Greek	Latin	**Both**	Neither
tetrad	**Greek**	Latin	Both	Neither
usher	Greek	**Latin**	Both	Neither
venom	Greek	**Latin**	Both	Neither
warm	Greek	Latin	Both	**Neither**
X ray	Greek	Latin	Both	**Neither**
yogurt	Greek	Latin	Both	**Neither**
zodiac	Greek	Latin	**Both**	Neither

Tome Test
Note: Your words will be different, so your language counts will vary. This answer is for the ten words from *laser* to *last*.
Latin—3
Greek—0

King Toot's Hazardous Puzzle of Pain 2
p.66
1. First syllable

2. Two

3. Noun and verb

4. Two / adjective and adverb

5. Pyramidal, pyramidally, pyramidical

6. No

7. Latin and Greek

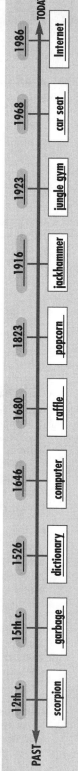

ANSWER PAGES

8. Yes / pyramid- or pyramis

9. An ancient massive structure found esp. in Egypt having a typ- ically square ground plan, out- side walls in the form of four tri- angles that meet in a point at the top, and inner sepulchral cham- bers.

10. To speculate (as on a securi- ty or commodity exchange) by using paper profits as margin for additional transactions. *(Note: your answer may be different.)*

Extra Hazardous Password 2

Percent

Chamber 3
World Atlas

(Using *Goode's World Atlas: 20th Edition* [Rand McNally])
Note: Your atlas may give *slightly* different latitudes and longitudes for these places. All atlases vary by a few degrees here and there.

Finding the Maps
p.70
KING TOOT'S TOMB
PAGE NUMBERS FOR THE MAPS OF AFRICA.
Pages: 225-238
PAGE NUMBER FOR A MAP OF EGYPT.
Page: 231
PAGE NUMBER FOR THE CITY OF MEMPHIS, EGYPT.
Page: 238b

TENNESSEE'S HOMETOWN
PAGE NUMBERS THE MAPS OF NORTH AMERICA.
Pages: 67-135

PAGE NUMBER FOR A MAP OF THE U.S.A.
Page: 104
PAGE NUMBER FOR A MAP OF TENNESSEE.
Page: 107
FIND THE PAGE NUMBER FOR MEMPHIS, TENNESSEE.
Page: 105

> ### Tome Test
> Number:4
> Memphis, Mo., U.S.
> Memphis, Tn., U.S.
> Memphis, Tx., U.S.
> Memphis, Egypt

Using the Index
p.72
Agri River
Agri, r., Italy.... **174** 40°15'N 16°21'E
PLACE   RIVER   COUNTRY   PAGE#   LATITUDE   LONGITUDE

Chandeleur Islands
Chandeleur Islands, is., La., U.S. .... **124** 29°53'N 88°35'W
PLACE   ISLAND   STATE   COUNTRY   PAGE#   LATITUDE   LONGITUDE

Ivory Coast
Ivory Coast, nation, Afr. **230** 7°43'N 6°30'W
PLACE   COUNTRY   CONTINENT   PAGE#   LATITUDE   LONGITUDE

Capitol Reef National Park
Capitol Reef Nat. Park, Ut., U.S. .... **119** 38°15'N 111°10'W
PLACE   STATE   COUNTRY   PAGE#   LATITUDE   LONGITUDE

North Dakota
North Dakota, state, U.S. **104** 47°20'N 101°55'W
PLACE   COUNTRY   PAGE#   LATITUDE   LONGITUDE

Midway Islands
Midway Islands, is. Oc....**2** 28°00'N 179°00'W
PLACE   COUNTRY   PAGE#   LATITUDE   LONGITUDE

> ### Tome Test
> c. Cape, Point
> vol. Volcano
> b. Bay, Gulf, Inlet, Lagoon

Map Coordinates
p.74
Grid Coordinates

Nashville	E2
Knoxville	H2
Memphis	B4
Shelbyville	E3
Watts Bar Lake	G3
Evansville	B2
Pulaski	D4
La Follette	H1
Milan	C3

Latitude and Longitude 1
p.76

	Approx Lat.	Exact Lat.
Seattle, WA	48°00'N	47°36'N
Portland, OR	46°00'N	45°31'N
Sacramento, CA	39°00'N	38°35'N
San Francisco, CA	38°00'N	37°45'N
Los Angeles, CA	34°00'N	34°03'N
San Diego, CA	33°00'N	32°43'N

	Approx Long.	Exact Long.
Columbus, OH	83°00'W	83°00'W
Cincinnati, OH	85°00'W	84°30'W
Indianapolis, IN	86 00'W	86°08'W
Chicago, IL	88°00'W	87°37'W
St. Louis, MO	90°00'W	90°15'W
Kansas City, MO	95°00'W	94°35'W

> ### Tome Test
> Because the 48 contiguous U.S. states are north of the equator and west of the Greenwich meridian.

Latitude and Longitude 2
p.78

	LATITUDE	LONGITUDE
Beijing, China	39°55'N	116°23'E
Delhi, India	28°54'N	77°13'E
Johannesburg, South Africa	26°08'S	27°54'E
London, England	51°30'N	00°07'W
Moscow, Russia	55°45'N	37°37'E
New York, NY	40°40'N	73°58'W
Paris, France	48°51'N	02°20'E
Tokyo, Japan	35°42'N	139°46'E
Furthest south?	Johannesburg	

Furthest north? Moscow
Furthest east? Tokyo
Furthest west? New York

Tome Test

	LATITUDE	LONGITUDE
Tobyhanna, Pa. (aunt)	41°11'N	75°25'W
Newburgh, Ind. (grandfather)	37°57'N	87°24'W
Mansfield, La. (friend)	32°02'N	93°43'W

Cities and Towns
p.80

California (Western U.S.)

Cities	Size
Santa Cruz	3
San Francisco	1
San Jose	2

Egypt (Nile Valley)

Cities	Size
Bani Suwayf	3
El Qahira	1
Al Minya	2

Cameroon (Central Africa)

Cities	Size
Douala	1
Yaounde	2
Kumba	3

Australia

Cities	Size
Newcastle	2
Wagga Wagga	3
Sydney	1

Alberta (Canada)

Cities	Size
Calgary	1
Olds	3
Red Deer	2

Tome Test
State: Tennessee
Cities: Newbern, Trenton, Milan

Scale and Distance
p.82
Scale: 1 inch = 100 miles
Palmdale to Felda: 2 1/2 inches = 250 miles
Columbus to Albany: 4 inches = 400 miles

Scale: 1 cm = 10 kilometers
Bern to Eggiwil: 4 cm = 40 km
Cork to Cobh: 2.5 cm = 25 km

Scale: 1 cm = 250 miles
Riyadh to Pavlodar: 9 cm = 2,250 miles

Tome Test

Scale	Map Distance	Real Distance
1 inch = 50 miles	10 1/2 in	525 miles
1 cm = 1,200 miles	3 cm	3,600 miles

Physical Features
p.84
Physical Features Key

Airfield   Ruin

Salt water   Point of Interest

GREENLAND
Ice caps and glaciers
HUNGARY
Balaton
SOUTH DAKOTA
Badlands National Park
NILE VALLEY
Ruins or Archeological Sites

Tome Test
Four:
Fresh Water
Fresh Water: Intermittent
Salt Water
Salt Water: Intermittent

Physical Features 2
p.86
1. Major/Principal
2. Railroad
3. No
4. Both are on the same freshwater lake (Lake Michigan)
5. Other or secondary
6. Freshwater
7. Wabash and Ohio rivers
8. No
9. Yes
10. Cincinnati

Tome Test
Illinois, Kentucky, Ohio, Michigan

Elevation and Depth
p.88
Australia
Bass Strait
0-152.5 meters / 0-500 feet below sea level

South Australia
0-152.5 meters / 0-500 meters above sea level

Indian Ocean
3,050-10,000 meters / 10,000-20,000 feet below sea level

Mt. Zeil
1,510 meters / 4,955 feet above sea level

Tajikistan/Central Asia
Tajikistan's Pamir range
over 3,050 meters / over 10,000 feet above sea level

What color represents this map's highest elevations?
White

Town of Dushanbe
610-1,525 meters / 2,000-5,000 feet above sea level

Mt. Pik Kommunizma
7,495 meters / 24,590 feet above sea level

Tome Test
B. Mountainous

World Maps Physical
p.90
1. Andes Mountains
2. Ice
3. more than 6,100 meters / 20,000 feet deep
4. Actual Lat./Long. 37 52's, 77 32'ᴇ
5. Mediterranean Sea
6. over 3,050 meters/10,000 feet tall
7. Selection of places on the equator:
Congo Basin (Africa)
Mt. Kenya (Africa)
Sumatra
Borneo
Gilbert Islands (Pacific Ocean)
Galapagos Island (Pacific Ocean)
Amazon River (South America)
8. Hudson Bay
9. North
10. Number: 4
Arctic, Atlantic, Pacific, Indian

Tome Test

	Size Ranking
Africa	2
Antarctica	5
Asia	1
Australia	7
Europe	6
North America	3
South America	4

World Maps Political
p.92
1. Brazil
2. Australia
3. North America
4. Pacific Ocean
5. Asia
6. Africa
7. Greenland
8. Canada
9. Jakarta
10. New Zealand

Tome Test
Argentina	Guyana
Bolivia	Paraguay
Brazil	Peru
Chile	Surinam
Colombia	Uruguay
Ecuador	Venezuela
French Guiana	

North America and the U.S.A.
p.94
1. Lake Superior
Lake Huron
Lake Erie
Lake Ontario
2. United States
3. West

4. Approx.   Exact
45⁰ɴ, 67⁰w   45⁰11ɴ, 67⁰17w
                      (Calais, Maine)
5. Pacific Ocean
6. Country: Russia
Continent: Asia
7. Mississippi River
8. 0-152.5 meters / 0-500 feet deep
9. Arctic Ocean, Atlantic Ocean
10. Denver, CO

Tome Test
North/South	East/West
Cleveland	Washington, D.C.
Salt Lake City	Cleveland
Washington, D.C.	Salt Lake City

Extra Hazardous Password Question 3

Vegetable

King Toot's Hazardous Puzzle of Pain 3
p.96

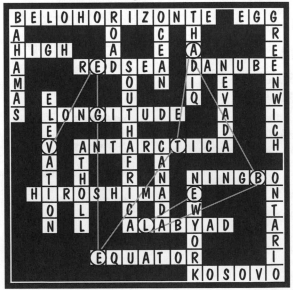

Chamber 4
Thesaurus

(Using *Roget's International Thesaurus: Sixth Edition*)

Thesaurus Basics
p.100

	Synonym	#	Name
moisture	rain	316.1	Rain
car	railway car	179.15	Vehicle
lounge	idle	331.12	Inactivity
chase	hunt	382.9	Pursuit
free	detach	802.10	Separation
cat	feline	311.21	Animals, Insects
skin	cheat	759.26	Gambling
surprise	attack	459.14	Attack
weight	boxer	754.2	Boxing

Word Classes
p.102
Chapter One
The Body and The Senses
3 Subcategories: Unclothing
Fragrance
Cleanness
Chapter Two: Feelings
3 Subcategories: Love
Cheerfulness
Hope
Chapter Three:
Place and Change of Place
3 Subcategories: Arrival
Town, City
Sea, Ocean
Chapter Four:
Behavior and Will
3 Subcategories: Obedience
Carefulness
Improvement
Chapter Five:
Human Society and Institutions
3 Subcategories: Marriage
Friendship
Public Spirit
Chapter Six:
Values and Ideals
3 Subcategories: Right
Honor
Moderation

Chapter Seven:
Science and Technology
3 Subcategories: Light
Automation
Space Travel

Tome Test
Any three of the following:
Measure and Shape
Living Things
Natural Phenomena
Language
Arts
Occupations and Crafts
Sports and Amusements
The Mind and Ideas

Using the Index 1
p.104

	Category.Paragraph #
salad	
1. food	10.37
2. hodgepodge	797.6
green	
1. *n* greenness	44.1
2. verdigris	44.3
jump	
1. *n* progression	162.1
2. step	177.11
ascend	
1. move	172.5
2. climb	184.39
mad	
1. *n* anger	152.5
2. *v* madden	926.24
bowl	
1. *n* tableware	8.12
2. cavity	284.2

Tome Test
WORD CLASS

salad	The Body and Senses
green	The Body and Senses
jump	Behavior and Will
ascend	Place and Change of Place
mad	Feelings
bowling	Sports and Amusements

Using the Index 2
p.106
Chapter 4:
Behavior and Will: Ruling My Empire With Class

After I returned from my sailing vacation down the Euphrates River, I had a country to run. My parents had been poisoned by an evil servant, so it was my turn to **rule** (<u>lead</u>) the **country** (<u>nation</u>). **Ruling** (<u>Commanding</u>) a **country** (<u>kingdom</u>) is very hard work. My father, King Froot, had a very hard time **ruling** (<u>supervising</u>) the **country** (<u>land</u>), so I knew it wouldn't be easy. The first thing I did was to name a new holiday after myself. I called the new **holiday** (<u>day off</u>) "Tootmas" and decreed that every year until the end of time, Tootmas would be a **holiday** (<u>festival day</u>) celebrated on the day I was crowned king.

My loyal subjects were all very happy. In fact, I had never seen them so **happy** (<u>glad</u>). They were usually sad because they had to give me so much of their money, and if they didn't, I would have them thrown in jail or fed to the lions. But Tootmas was a **happy** (<u>joyful</u>) **holiday** (<u>feast day</u>)! Men, women, and children lined the streets for the big parade past the pyramids. It was biggest parade Egypt had ever seen. There were **big** (<u>large</u>) statues carried on **big** (<u>immense</u>) platforms and **big** (<u>gigantic</u>) tables full of food and drinks. At the end of the parade, my royal jester Mel Boinks gave a comedy concert called *Boinks A lot!* It was very funny. Mel Boinks can be **very** (<u>exceedingly</u>) **funny** (<u>amusing</u>) when he sets his mind to it.

I was **very** (<u>quite</u>) pleased with the concert — until Boinks told a joke about my tiny feet. Just because my **feet** (<u>dogs</u>) are the size of a baby's doesn't mean he can **joke** (<u>kid around</u>) about them!

ANSWER PAGES

So I had him put in a cage and I gave people feathers so they could tickle him until he cried. Now that was **funny** (<u>delightful</u>)!

Tome Test

COUNTRY	BIG
1. state	1. enormous
2. empire	2. titanic
3. realm	3. massive

Choosing the Best Synonym
p.108

Word	Good Synonyms
food	cuisine, fare, chow, grub
sad	unhappy, heavy hearted, depressed, down
future	hereafter, beyond, distant future
possess	have, own, command
facts	particulars, details, specifics, data
new	fresh, original, modern, contemporary
help	aid, assist, succeed, prevail, deliver, come through
friend	companion, comrade, pal, buddy
tomb	crypt, vault, catacombs, mummy chamber

Tome Test
Food: enchilada

Descriptive Words	Best Synonym
1. spicy	peppery
2. tasty	yummy
3. hot	steamy

King Toot's Hazardous Puzzle of Pain 4
p.110
I Was a Teenage Mummy
Synonyms
1. face
2. ajar
3. repeat
4. sheep
5. breathing
6. oil

Extra Hazardous Password 4

Oil

Extra Hazardous Password that Releases Tennessee!

TEN
PERCENT
VEGETABLE
OIL

CONGRATULATIONS!

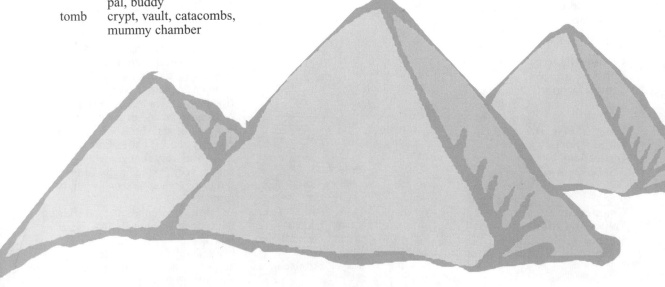